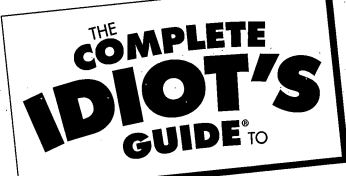

THE COMPLETE IDIOT'S GUIDE® TO

Conversational Sign Language

Illustrated

by Carole Lazorisak
Dawn Donohue

ALPHA

A member of Penguin Group (USA) Inc.

We dedicate this book to all hearing people who have taken the step to heighten their awareness, sensitivity, and understanding about deaf people and their life experiences. We thank you for breaking down the barriers between the Deaf world and hearing world and for opening up lines of communication. It is our hope that you will build relationships and be receptive to the differences of deaf people and their ways of communication.

ALPHA BOOKS

Published by the Penguin Group

Penguin Group (USA) Inc., 375 Hudson Street, New York, New York 10014, USA

Penguin Group (Canada), 90 Eglinton Avenue East, Suite 700, Toronto, Ontario M4P 2Y3, Canada (a division of Pearson Penguin Canada Inc.)

Penguin Books Ltd., 80 Strand, London WC2R 0RL, England

Penguin Ireland, 25 St. Stephen's Green, Dublin 2, Ireland (a division of Penguin Books Ltd.)

Penguin Group (Australia), 250 Camberwell Road, Camberwell, Victoria 3124, Australia (a division of Pearson Australia Group Pty. Ltd.)

Penguin Books India Pvt. Ltd., 11 Community Centre, Panchsheel Park, New Delhi—110 017, India

Penguin Group (NZ), 67 Apollo Drive, Rosedale, North Shore, Auckland 1311, New Zealand (a division of Pearson New Zealand Ltd.)

Penguin Books (South Africa) (Pty.) Ltd., 24 Sturdee Avenue, Rosebank, Johannesburg 2196, South Africa

Penguin Books Ltd., Registered Offices: 80 Strand, London WC2R 0RL, England

International Standard Book Number: 978-1-59257-255-7
Library of Congress Catalog Card Number: 2004106744

09   12 11

Interpretation of the printing code: The rightmost number of the first series of numbers is the year of the book's printing; the rightmost number of the second series of numbers is the number of the book's printing. For example, a printing code of 04-1 shows that the first printing occurred in 2004.

Printed in the United States of America

Note: This publication contains the opinions and ideas of its authors. It is intended to provide helpful and informative material on the subject matter covered. It is sold with the understanding that the authors and publisher are not engaged in rendering professional services in the book. If the reader requires personal assistance or advice, a competent professional should be consulted.

The authors and publisher specifically disclaim any responsibility for any liability, loss, or risk, personal or otherwise, which is incurred as a consequence, directly or indirectly, of the use and application of any of the contents of this book.

Most Alpha books are available at special quantity discounts for bulk purchases for sales promotions, premiums, fund-raising, or educational use. Special books, or book excerpts, can also be created to fit specific needs.

For details, write: Special Markets, Alpha Books, 375 Hudson Street, New York, NY 10014.

Publisher: *Marie Butler-Knight*
Product Manager: *Phil Kitchel*
Senior Managing Editor: *Jennifer Chisholm*
Senior Acquisitions Editor: *Mike Sanders*
Senior Development Editor: *Tom Stevens*
Senior Production Editor: *Billy Fields*
Copy Editor: *Jan Zoya*
Photographer: *Erik Olson*
Illustrator: *Richard King*
Cover/Book Designer: *Trina Wurst*
Indexer: *Tonya Heard*
Layout/Proofreading: *Mary Hunt, Trina Wurst*
Graphics: *Tammy Graham*

Contents at a Glance

Contents

Table of Signs

Foreword

Communication is essential to understanding the world. Historically, in America, deaf and hearing people have struggled to communicate with one another. This has been a challenging endeavor, often resulting in misunderstandings, but the act of communication whether through gesture, writing, or pantomime illustrates the desire to connect. This book begins the process of melding two worlds efficiently and skillfully through Contact Signing.

Contact Signing (CS) is a tool that satisfies the need to communicate, occurring when two divergent speakers, deaf and hearing, meet and mediate the interaction with aspects of the other's language properties. Word order tends to follow spoken English rather than grammatical rules of American Sign Language (ASL). Notwithstanding, the process of visual communication is fascinating, in that all hearing people from all cultures incorporate natural gesture with the spoken form. Think of the natural gestures in the United States for "okay." Whether one chooses "thumbs up," or uses pointer and thumb to create a circle with the middle, ring, and pinkie fingers extended, it is understood. Therefore, visual forms of communication can create equivalent meaning without voice. Learning to use CS will enhance your awareness of the visual tendencies we all possess.

Sign Language, created by deaf people for deaf people, is an exquisite, complex language. "... So long as there are two deaf people upon the face of the earth, ... will signs be in use." (J. Schuyler Long, 1910). Acknowledging this, the authors' intent is to excite you, enticing you to explore the possibility of communicating with someone who uses language visually. While ASL is a vibrant language, becoming fluent, knowledgeable, and respectful of Deaf culture requires many years of study and interaction. Carole and Dawn created this primer to whet your appetite, offering an opportunity to learn a functional system of communication that will facilitate daily interaction with your neighbor, family member, customer, or co-worker, hopefully leading to further study and cross-cultural exploration.

I have been extremely fortunate to be a colleague and friend of Carole Lazorisak since 1989. We have collaborated often professionally, presenting together at conferences locally, nationally, and internationally, and over the years our personal lives have touched and become family. Carole's uncanny ability to transcend spoken language in the many countries she has visited alone or with friends and family is testament that the need to communicate and understand is an integral part of one's being. Her daughter, Dawn, is testament that mother-daughter bonds are dynamic and complimentary, a never-ending learning process.

This journey via Contact Signing will catapult you into a new perspective of the world. In conjunction, Carole and Dawn articulate aspects of Deaf community, language, and lifestyle, providing an overview of the richness of this world, paving your way to communicating with people who are deaf. Open your eyes and mind to a mother-daughter team who will guide you into the realm of visual communication.

—Janice B. Rimler, M.Ed., RID: CT, ASLTA: Professional, Adjunct Professor and Coordinator of Interpreter Services, New York City College of Technology/CUNY

Introduction

The main goal of this book is to help facilitate conversations in sign language, particularly conversations between deaf and hearing persons. Our readers are those who wish to communicate with deaf people in an easy manner, for simple conversations, in a variety of scenarios. The book was written to be used as a tool and a resource toward bridging the gap between the deaf and hearing worlds. We encourage the initiation of dialogue, and—most important—keeping the lines of communication open for continuous dialogues!

This book does not teach American Sign Language (ASL), which is used primarily by deaf people among themselves and by professional sign interpreters or teachers. It is not intended to teach you all the signs (there are plenty of ASL dictionary books out there for that) or the complex grammatical structure (there are books out there for this, too). Nor does this book teach Signed English (SE), which is often used by educators who wish to teach English as a first language to deaf children and adults.

This book teaches a form of communication called Contact Signing (formerly known for many years as Pidgin Sign English). Contact Signing (CS) has grown to become the most widely used form of communication between hearing people and deaf people in America when they come together to communicate. CS is a natural outcome developing as a result of two language users (those who speak English and those who use ASL) making "contact" with one another and negotiating the communication. This results in "borrowing" from each language to create an understandable communication. The world is becoming "smaller," and people from all walks of life are interacting daily, learning about each other's languages and cultures. Contact Signing is also becoming more popular in its usage between deaf people as well. CS is easy to learn, and you'll have plenty of support along the way, with lots of explanations and photo illustrations in this book, as well as a DVD to show you what to sign and how to sign it!

The authors also aim to give you a better idea of what it's like to be deaf and to live in a hearing-majority world. We begin this book by sharing with you some FAQs we've collected over the years from hearing people wanting to know about the differences (and similarities) shared. How many deaf Americans are there? Can deaf people drive? Can they use a phone? What is the Deaf culture? What's the difference between the two terms "Deaf" and "deaf"? What is sign language and who uses it? Is sign language the same all over the world? As we answer these questions, you'll come to know why the Deaf culture is strong and close-knit, and how special it is to be accepted into this community. And we'll provide you with information, stories, facts, and interesting tidbits so you will have a better understanding of the "Deaf experience."

Another aspiration of this book is to teach you some fundamental vocabulary and common sentences that you may use often for simple and basic signed conversations in everyday scenarios. Unlike many books that only teach you signs, we've put signs together to form familiar phrases you can use interchangeably in various settings as needs arise. We also explain how to use your face and body along with your hands in order to enhance your communication.

All of this will put you well on your way to signing confidently with deaf people and having sensitive and basic conversations. It may seem like a lot to learn, but don't worry, we'll help you get there! So, relax and have fun!

Your journey into the world of the deaf begins in **Part 1, "Overview of Deafness."** Carole and Dawn will cover important topics that you need to know, including medical and cultural perspectives of deafness, culture, language and communication. We answer frequently asked questions from hearing people about Deaf life experiences, abilities, and daily routines.

You prepare yourself for signing in **Part 2, "Getting Ready to Sign—Express Yourself!"** You learn signing etiquette and what to do and not do when you're face to face with a deaf person. Hand formations and positioning, facial expressions, body movements, and use of physical space are all also discussed here.

Give your hands a workout as you learn and practice signs in **Part 3, "Essential Basic Signs."** You learn fingerspelling and signs that you'll use every day, such as the American Manual Alphabet, numbers, and colors.

Parts 4 through 6 all have conversational vignettes—These are commonly used sentences and phrases, presented within a variety of scenarios. **Part 4, "Getting To Know You,"** teaches greetings, light discourse, and conversation endings that you can use in many formal and informal situations. **Part 5, "Getting To Know More About You,"** features signs you use at a party, work, school, visiting someone's home, in a restaurant, or out shopping. **Part 6, "Thanks for Your Help!,"** covers important signs to communicate with deaf people when someone's lost, sick, in trouble with the law, or in a fire emergency. The book shows photographs (with movement directives) of Carole and Dawn as they sign the Contact Signing dialogues. Carole will also show you additional and interchangeable signs. On the DVD, you'll see hands in motion as Carole and Dawn sign to each other and then as Carole teaches you individual signs.

Part 7, "You're Off and Signing!," features the last signing chapter, showing signs and tips you use to make sure your conversation is on track, and if it isn't, you'll know what to ask and do to get it back! We end the book with information on how to practice and fine-tune what you've already learned, as well as point you to resources that can help to continue your journey.

You'll also encounter the following extras throughout the book:

Sign On _____

Sign Ons are things that you should know as you learn about Deaf culture and other topics. They're pieces of positive information and also tips that further explain how to make a sign.

Sign Off _____

Sign Offs, conversely, are pieces of information that show misconceptions and other things to avoid. Sign Offs are used also to alert you to what not to do when forming a sign.

Sign Post _____

Bet you didn't know! These boxes will share interesting facts, pieces of interesting information, facts, stories, and quotes.

ON THE DVD

This logo is to remind you to refer to DVD to see the chapter's signs in action. Have fun signing along with Carole and Dawn!

Acknowledgments

Gratitudes go to literary agent Marilyn Allen from the Allen O'Shea Literary Agency and to Mike Sanders from Alpha Books for their belief and support in our mission and for helping to make this book become a reality. We give a huge thanks to Ascent Media, especially to Adam Tronik and his fabulous team who did an awesome job taping and producing (Andrew Eichhorn, Mike Hull, George Greczylo), editing (Russ Combs), authoring (Alan Gavin) and manufacturing (Greg Whitehouse) the DVD; and to Ascent's Erik Olsen for his excellent photography. Much thanks go to Margaret Durante for sharing her terrific and animated voice!

We also thank our friends, students, and colleagues for all their story contributions and expertise. We appreciate their invaluable input and encouragement during the book development and writing. Special thanks go to Janice B. Rimler and Katherine Dudina.

Thanks to Carole's husband Andy for his hard work on all the photo "sign-movement directives" for this book and for his expertise during the DVD editing process. Thanks to Dawn's husband, Mark, for all his love and support and to Mark and the Donohue family and Kircher family for inspiring parts of this book. Special note to all—Mark learned enough conversational signs to communicate with Dawn's parents the first time he met them, after just three months of dating! And to son/brother Paul, thank you for being you and for your advice. We love you all!

Trademarks

All terms mentioned in this book that are known to be or are suspected of being trademarks or service marks have been appropriately capitalized. Alpha Books and Penguin Group (USA) Inc. cannot attest to the accuracy of this information. Use of a term in this book should not be regarded as affecting the validity of any trademark or service mark.

In This Part

Part 1

Overview of Deafness

We begin with an overview of the Deaf experience and culture to give you insight into being deaf and topics of deafness. History, culture, abilities, achievements, needs, education, language, and technology are all touched on here. We hope to clarify any misconceptions, and do so in an honest way. We have chosen topics based on frequently asked questions from hearing people.

It should be noted that although there are varied degrees of deafness or any hearing loss, we will refer to those with hearing loss as "deaf" for purposes of this book.

In This Chapter

- ◆ Degrees of hearing loss
- ◆ Causes of deafness
- ◆ Our fellow deaf Americans
- ◆ Hearing aids
- ◆ Deaf culture

    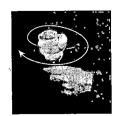

Chapter 1

The Basics of Deafness

So what would it be like to be deaf and live in a foreign hearing world full of sounds? You wouldn't hear your significant other say "I love you." Or hear your child call your name. Or listen to various notes and instruments playing beautiful classical music, or lyrics of a hard-rock song. You wouldn't hear someone behind you repeat "excuse me" several times before she forcefully pushed you out of her way. You wouldn't hear a microwave beeping to tell you that your food has been cooked, or a running faucet about to overflow. And you wouldn't hear someone warn you to "watch out" before a biker zoomed right in front of you. And would people try to communicate with you or leave you feeling left out?

In this chapter, we explore what it means to be deaf—from a medical viewpoint to a cultural one. We look at the reasons people become deaf, what it's like to be deaf, and the Deaf community and culture.

How Many Deaf Americans Are There?

No one really knows for sure how many deaf Americans there are. Some demographic statistics are available, but because there are varied degrees of hearing loss, some people may or may not identify themselves as deaf. Further throwing off statistics is the fact that some people who classify themselves as "deaf" may actually be hard-of-hearing, and some "hard-of-hearing" people may actually be deaf.

Sign Post

According to a study of 43,000 deaf children (aged 1–18) across the United States by the Gallaudet Research Institute in 2002, 84 percent of deaf children have parents who are hearing. Seventy-two percent of these children reported that their family members do not regularly sign to them.

In a report by the National Center for Health Statistics (NCHS) released December 2000, 17 percent of the U.S. adult population experienced some level of hearing loss. It was noted that men were somewhat more likely to experience hearing loss than women. Regionally, adults in the Midwest were more likely to experience hearing loss than adults in the South and Northeast. While most of the adult population with hearing loss are those who have lost hearing with age, approximately 12 out of every 1,000 persons with hearing loss is under 18 years of age. In an earlier report released in 1994, the NCHS reported that only 4.5 million Americans (a small percentage of the total number with hearing loss) were using assistive technology for hearing loss.

Sign On

According to the National Association of the Deaf in 2003, there are over 28 million Americans who have some degree of hearing loss. Some other studies estimate that number to be approximately 34 million.

Do All Deaf People Hear Nothing?

We can all agree that to be "deaf" means that you may not have the ability to hear sounds of speech. But, there are actually varied degrees of deafness.

Sound is measured by decibels (dB). People who are deaf have a severe (60–95dB) or profound (over 90dB) hearing loss. This means that they may hear loud sounds such as a lawn mower or an airplane at 1,000 feet, but may not have the ability to hear speech.

People who are hard-of-hearing have a mild to moderate hearing loss (25–60dB). It is possible that they can hear some sounds (including speech) through the use of technology such as hearing aids or other assistive listening devices (which amplify sounds).

The following are points of reference for sounds in decibels(dB):

- ◆ 0dB: The softest sound a person can hear with normal hearing
- ◆ 10dB: Normal breathing
- ◆ 20dB: Whispering at five feet
- ◆ 30dB: Soft whisper
- ◆ 50dB: Rainfall
- ◆ 60dB: Normal conversation
- ◆ 110dB: Shouting in ear
- ◆ 120dB: Thunder

How Does Someone Become Deaf?

There are different reasons why someone may be deaf. A person may have been born deaf, or have experienced a quick or slow loss of hearing over time. Genetics, diseases, ear infections, noise, accidents, earwax buildup, and certain medications can all come into play here.

Sign Off _____

> Deafness is not "contagious." It's not a disease that you can catch from someone else.

Sometimes hearing losses result from illnesses. In our family's case, Andrew had a fever that became so severe it permanently damaged his inner-ear functions. Lou Ferrigno, the "Hulk" actor from the popular *Incredible Hulk* television series in the late '70s and '80s, suffered an 85 percent hearing loss due to having an ear infection at a young age. But he didn't let this stop him! He has since been featured in over 15 movies and played professional football for the Toronto Argonauts. Lou initially gained his fame by winning bodybuilding titles, such as Mr. America and Mr. International. By the time he was 21, he was the youngest athlete to ever win the Mr. Universe title, a Guinness Book record that has yet to be broken.

Sign Post _____

> Lou Ferrigno was quoted as saying, "If I hadn't lost my hearing, I wouldn't be where I am now. It forced me to maximize my own potential. I have to be better than the average person to succeed."

Gradual hearing loss, called presbycusis, is especially common in older adults. It is a progressive loss of the ability to hear higher frequencies, such as human speech. According to a 2002 report by Steven Angelo, M.D., at the Yale School of Medicine, hearing loss interferes with social interaction in 25 percent of adults ages 65 to 75, and in 70 to 80 percent of adults age 75 and older. Over the next two decades, as the "baby boomer" generation reaches these ages, we're sure to see more and more people with hearing loss—another good reason to start learning some signs!

Sign Off _____

> Noise levels above 85dB will harm hearing over time. Noise levels above 140dB can cause damage to hearing after just one exposure.

Sometimes hearing loss is caused by exposure to loud noises. In 1997, former President Bill Clinton was fitted for hearing aids during his presidency, at the age of 51. Doctors concluded that his hearing loss was caused partly due to age, and partly due to exposure to loud noises—especially from musical instruments. President Clinton attributed his hearing loss to noisy rock concerts he attended as a teenager, and also from the loud music he played while performing on his saxophone.

Sign Post _____

> According to the Musician's Clinics of Canada, 37 percent of rock musicians and 52 percent of classical musicians are affected by at least some degree of hearing loss. There is hearing loss reported by 60 percent of rock stars inducted into the Rock and Roll Hall of Fame, from continued exposure to sounds over 110dB.

Can All Deaf People "Hear" by Using Hearing Aids or Other Ear Devices?

Placed in the ear, hearing aids are electronic devices with a small microphone that amplifies sounds through a small speaker. A person must have some ability to hear for the device to work. Because hearing loss affects people in different levels, some people find hearing aids to be more helpful than others.

It is important to understand that hearing aids only amplify existing sounds. They do not "restore hearing." Contrary to popular belief, they cannot clarify speech for deaf people, which is a common complaint. Additionally, since hearing aids intensify all sounds, the amplification of background noise is also a frequent problem.

Sign Post

Barbara Dale, a deaf woman who lives in New York, says that, "Hearing aids are wonderful if you are able to discriminate sounds. But, sometimes they amplify background sounds or noises that could be very intolerable, such as whistling, screeching of brakes, or chattering of crowds."

While hearing aids are temporary, removable devices to assist amplification of sound, a topic of great controversy in the Deaf community is cochlear implants. Cochlear implants, also known as "bionic ears," are hoped to activate auditory nerve fibers allowing for the transmission of sound signals to the brain. Common to all cochlear implants is a bundle of fine wires (like a spiral tube) that are surgically implanted into the hearing portion of the inner ear—the cochlea. An external device includes a sound processor, a cable, and a microphone that is housed in a headpiece. As of August, 2003, over 60,000 implantations have been performed worldwide. Most procedures have been done on young deaf children.

Cochlear implants differ from hearing aids. Hearing aids simply makes sounds louder. Cochlear implants directly stimulate nerve cells in the inner ear. It is currently still difficult for surgeons and doctors to predict the potential benefit for a patient receiving a cochlear implant. There is also a risk for meningitis due to possible "dead space" within the ear that could provide a home for infection and bacteria (according to Professor Graeme Clark, the inventor of the implants). In May 2003, the FDA stated that they had learned of 118 cases of cochlear implant recipients worldwide who developed bacterial meningitis. The auditory nerve fibers, structural damage, and duration of hearing loss may all influence the performance of an implant. However, researchers are still evaluating these factors.

Sign Post

Dennis Dale, the husband of Barbara Dale of New York, was classified as deaf and was one of the first to receive a cochlear implant, over 20 years ago. He says, "I have gained back only some residual hearing and I wish that I could understand and discriminate speech. However, I have no regrets in getting this wonderful technology."

What's It Like to Be Deaf?

Just as each hearing person has different experiences in his or her life, so does a deaf person. But in addition to life challenges that hearing people have, deaf people will, at some point, additionally experience levels of frustration, communication problems, and feelings of isolation or exclusion.

Carole invites you to go on a journey with her into her Deaf world and learn more about what it is like to be deaf yet live in a hearing world filled with sounds. Let's start the day in a Deaf home …

"It is 6:00 A.M. and the alarm clock is flashing by the bedside. I wake up and turn off the alarm. From my bed, I look out the window to see what the weather is like. What is the sky showing? Is it a clear or a rainy day? How are the leaves and branches moving? I rely on my eyes to give me information and to help me figure out what's going on. This is how every day begins!

"I walk down the stairs and am greeted by our pet dog and bird. Our pets are our "ears" for us, and we can read their body movements and expressions to be alerted to strange sounds outside (such as a stranger walking up to the door). The dog knows that I am deaf and it has been taught signs such as COME-HERE, SIT-DOWN, and STAY. The dog knows to come up to me when it is hungry or wants to go out to the bathroom. The dog and bird are quiet now, so I know there's no one coming by and I can get ready to leave for work.

"I head toward the door—toward the world of sounds and to the world of ignorance. My neighbor waves at me with a smile and I return the gesture—this is our way of saying good-morning to each other.

"I drive to the food market. People do not see me as different. As I walk up and down the aisle, sometimes I stop to read the labels on packages. Sometimes people come up behind me and say, "Excuse me." They might repeat this several times and then become angry when I don't move, thinking that I am being rude. But, it's only because I don't hear them or have not seen them peripherally. By the time I put the package back on the shelf, I turn around and am startled and puzzled by their behavior. I didn't even know someone was behind me to begin with!

"I've had more than a few unpleasant experiences when strangers asked me to move. One day I was in a bookstore reviewing a book and a man pushed me hard and walked past me angrily. I was upset even though I knew this was a common behavioral pattern of hearing people. You can't tell that I'm deaf just from "looking" at me! The result? Sometimes people become impatient, annoyed, and verbally or physically abusive.

"Some of the questions often asked by strangers are: 'Can you drive?' ('I'm deaf, not blind,' is my thought to this question!), and 'How do you have a baby?' ("Just like every other human being," I think to myself). Many other questions that amaze me are: 'How do you teach your children to talk?' 'How did you buy a house?' 'How do you travel around the world?' 'How do you get around if you do not speak with your voice?' 'Why do you talk funny?' 'Is there something wrong with your voice?' and 'How do you teach hearing people?'

"Every day I face the hearing world—in the neighborhood, on the roadway, at the stores, at work, and other places. I see people talking but do not understand what they are saying. I see people laughing, and I do not know why they are laughing. I see people cry, and I do not know why they are upset. I see people with mouths opening and closing rapidly without the use of gesturing and do not know what is happening. However, when people use gestures and their visual communication is clear, I feel welcomed into their world. Typically, these people have an open mind and accept people who are 'different.' It is not about words or sounds—it is about forming relationships with humans of difference.

"Every day I know that in some way I will face ignorance, oppression, and discrimination—basically because I am different. Communication with hearing people is a daily battle. They do not know if I can use my voice, and, what if I do? My voice and speech is not clear to the ears of hearing people. Many hearing people seem afraid to communicate with me. Hearing people may be afraid to use gestures—afraid that they will make a mistake and not gesture correctly, or afraid that they will look like a fool communicating that way. Some people seem afraid to pick up a pen and paper to write a note to me. Do they think I can't read or write?

"I have been deaf from birth and it was a great struggle to learn English, which is a sound-based language. Learning English was very tasking, because letters, words, and phrases had to be memorized. English does not come as naturally to me as it does for hearing people. Even today, I constantly read and study different aspects of English. New vocabulary, new phrases, and idioms are a great challenge! All these need to be memorized.

"I am proud to be deaf and I feel good that I am bi-lingual. I continue with my post-college studies and love to travel to different parts of the world. I find people overseas (especially in Europe) to be very receptive to the use of gesturing, and this makes communication easier. Here in America, I continue to educate hearing people about the beauty of the Deaf world, to see the world with a new set of eyes, and to encourage hearing people to use their body to communicate.

"I end my day by going back to my comfortable and familiar Deaf house, and feeling exhausted from a very long day being out of the home. I take my bird out of its cage so it can fly around. And, just like me, it is now free and free to be!

"I look out the window and see the glorious and colorful sunset. The sun gives off its radiant colors before it leaves the horizon of the earth. These colors are like music to my eyes—providing me with entertainment and beauty. The painting of the sky is like music singing "good byes" before the night comes."

Who Comprises the Deaf Community?

The Deaf community is made up of those who are deaf and share a common language, values, culture, and experiences.

Members of the Deaf community …

◆ Understand that deafness is not a disability.

◆ Are proud to be Deaf.

◆ Use American Sign Language to visually communicate.

◆ Associate with other deaf people.

◆ Are involved in Deaf culture.

Sign On _____

The Deaf community uses an initial uppercased "D" (Deaf) when referring to those who use American Sign Language and are a part of the Deaf culture. A lowercased "d" (deaf) is used when referring to the physical nature of deafness or as a generic term for deaf and hard-of-hearing people.

Sometimes hearing people can be accepted and welcomed into the Deaf community. You have to take steps first, and begin by getting involved with the deaf community at large (Note: this is "small d"—comprised of deaf and hard-of hearing people). To be a part of the larger deaf community, you'll need to have basic skills in sign language and understand deaf perspectives. As you build your experiences and gain fluency in ASL, you can begin to get involved with activities associated with the Deaf culture.

Things that you may do include the following:

◆ Learn sign language (e.g., study from books, take classes, practice with other signers).

◆ Go to Deaf events (e.g., social gatherings, conferences, and conventions).

◆ Learn about Deaf culture (e.g., read books, magazines, articles, newsletters, websites, art shows, plays, and get out there and socialize with deaf people).

◆ Volunteer at local public-school Deaf programs in your area and ask to meet with teachers, interpreters, and other professionals who work with deaf children.

Sign Post _____

You can learn about Deaf events that are going on in your area from the website www.deafmall.net/events/. They have listings of Deaf events taking place across America and around the world!

What Is "Deaf Culture"?

Many deaf people are proud to be deaf, and they wouldn't want to be hearing. Hearing people may be amazed that some people prefer to be deaf. They may wonder: Why wouldn't all deaf people rather be hearing if given the chance? As hard as it is for hearing people to believe, many deaf people consider themselves lucky because of the enriching and rewarding experiences unique to Deaf culture.

Sign Off _____

Deaf people may feel "left out" of hearing populations. They may experience that some hearing people seem to be hesitant or uncomfortable in communicating with them. Given this, deaf people may seek each other out for social interaction and support.

How does Deaf culture develop?

◆ Similar, common language (ASL)

◆ Common learning and life experiences

◆ Shared visual-learning styles

◆ Friends and contacts within the Deaf community

◆ Interactions with other Deaf in schools, clubs, or societies

◆ Shared experience of being part of a minority group marginalized by society

There is a common sense of pride among many deaf people. There exists a rich heritage within the Deaf culture that recognizes its ability to overcome adversity as individuals and as a group. The Deaf culture has its own values, rules of behavior, stories, art, and traditions. An essential part of Deaf culture is linked together by its unique language—American Sign Language (ASL).

Using ASL to tell stories is highly valued in Deaf culture. In this way, a common sense of Deaf values and experiences can be passed down through generations. ASL enables deaf people to express their thoughts and feelings freely in a language readily understood by each other. They can share common opinions and experiences from school, growing up, family ties, social events, and other life experiences and challenges. It's this language that highly contributes to a having pride in the Deaf "identity." Some deaf people are highly protective of their culture, while others are more accepting to allow hearing people to participate in learning from them. One's openness to letting outsiders into the Deaf culture is unique to every deaf individual and depends largely on the level of feelings of discrimination or oppression that he or she may have experienced through life from members of the hearing community.

Many deaf people (it is estimated at 90 percent) marry others who are deaf. Some deaf couples also wish for a deaf child so that they may pass on their heritage, values, and culture. Parents may choose that their deaf child attend a residential school, which provides a strong socialization and foundation in Deaf culture.

Sign Post

Mother, Father Deaf Day is observed on the last Sunday of April. Its purpose is to give Children of Deaf Adults (CODA) the opportunity to honor their deaf parents and to recognize the gifts of culture and language they received.

A powerful bonding force in the Deaf community is a Deaf club. It is in this setting that a deaf person can meet and socialize with other deaf individuals to enjoy conversation, sports and leisure, and entertainment. They share values, customs, ASL, stories, jokes, and history. They may even share ASL poetry, which is regarded as a beautiful way to see words in motion. As face-to-face communication is important in the Deaf community, Deaf clubs provide a forum for them to interact in a way to keep their culture alive.

Sign On

The 2002 Deaf Way International Conference and Festival was a week-long event held in Washington, D.C., which hosted thousands of people from all over the world to share and celebrate the "way of the Deaf." It welcomed all deaf and hearing who wished to learn about experiences of deaf people through various presentations, speakers, plays, and performances. For more information about this conference and possible future conferences, visit this website: www.deafway.org.

Deaf Theatre is also gaining in popularity and fills the void for deaf actors and audiences. Great literature and adaptations of classic, contemporary, and original works are brought to life using sign language. The National Theatre for the Deaf, established in 1967, brought sign language out of the shadows and placed it in the world spotlight, raising it to the level of an art form. Actors combining sign language and spoken English (a double-sensory experience) expand the boundaries of theatrical expression to the delight of deaf and hearing audiences alike. Now Deaf community members are able to laugh at the same comedies, cry at the same tragedies, and rub elbows in the same theatre lobbies as hearing audiences.

>
> **Sign Post** _____
> The Deaf West Theatre Company,
> established in 1991, has become
> very successful in a short time.
> Working with the Roundabout Theatre
> Company (NY), they combined deaf and
> hearing actors for the release of a hit play
> called, "Big River: The Adventures of
> Huckleberry Finn." This play was very suc-
> cessful in its 2003 run, receiving awards
> and publicity, and it even made it to
> Broadway in New York City.

The Deaf culture is strong, and deaf people often look upon other members of the Deaf community as role models. Deaf pageants are just one way to find role models who exemplify Deaf culture. The Miss Deaf America Pageant started in 1972 and had only five contestants—now it has hundreds who compete every year. According to the Miss Deaf America Program, the pageant began to achieve its main objective of "… a new concept to help us elevate the image and self-concept of deaf ladies through-out the United States. This is not an ordinary contest … beauty, poise, gracefulness are desir-able qualities, but the biggest point is one's cultural talent performance." There are pageants for younger deaf people, too. Since 1999, the Mr. and Miss Deaf Teen America Pageant provides opportunities for boys and girls ages 13 to 19 from Schools for the Deaf across the United States to have a wonderful opportunity to display their leadership skills, talents, fellowship, and congeniality.

There is a Deaf Olympics, called the Deaflympic Games. In January 2005, Mel-bourne, Australia, will host approximately 3,500 deaf athletes from over 90 countries in a 12-day sports and cultural festival. Fifteen individual and team sporting events will take place, including basketball, tennis, cycling, football, table tennis, marathon, volleyball, and water polo. The Deaflympic Games, under the patronage of the International Olympic Committee, is the second oldest multisport and cultural festival on Earth with a long and proud history since the Inaugural Games in Paris in 1924.

> **Sign On** _____
> The most recent Deaflympics was held
> in Rome, Italy, in 2001. After the 2005
> event in Melbourne, Australia, the next
> one will be hosted by Taipei, Taiwan, in
> 2009.

The Least You Need to Know

- There are over 28 million people in the United States with some degree of hear-ing loss.
- Deaf people have varied degrees of hear-ing loss. Depending on their level of hearing, they are classified as being deaf or hard-of-hearing.
- Most of the adult population with hearing loss has gradually lost their hearing due to old age.
- Many deaf people have experienced feel-ings of frustration, isolation, adversity, and exclusion from some in the hearing community.
- The Deaf community is united by a com-mon language, shared experiences, pride, and values.
- Deaf culture is very rich with its own tra-ditions, story-telling, art, poetry, clubs, sports events, and role models.

In This Chapter

- ◆ Education for deaf children and adults
- ◆ Everyday activities
- ◆ Deaf people and driving
- ◆ Special technologies used by deaf people

Chapter 2

Never Say Can't

The authors, one being deaf (mom, Carole) and one being hearing (daughter, Dawn), have had different experiences living in a hearing-majority community. As a hearing person, Dawn was never questioned about her abilities to live and function in the world. Society always thought that she could do things "normally," just like any other "normal" hearing person. Carole, however, continues to be challenged by erroneous perceived notions from some in the hearing community regarding what she can and can't do because of her deafness.

Over the years, Dawn has exposed hearing people (her friends, colleagues, fellow students, husband and extended family, and others) to Carole and the Deaf community. As many of Dawn's hearing associates did not have prior experience meeting a deaf person before Carole, they would ask her many questions regarding deaf peoples' abilities. Hearing person to hearing person, it was always easier just to ask Dawn about it than Carole. But some of the common questions indicate that more needs to be done to educate hearing people in the area of how deaf people live in a hearing-majority world. In this chapter, we look at the sensitive questions that hearing people commonly ask about deaf people's way of life. We hope to put some of those mis-conceived notions about deaf people's abilities to rest!

Do Deaf Children Have to Go to Special Schools?

In the past, deaf children were placed into special education classrooms with children of all disabilities. This is not the case today, and there are several options to consider for educating deaf children. Over the years there have been many heated debates on the best method of instruction—sign-language-based versus oral-based education. Many factors need to be considered, and which option a parent chooses should be based on the ideal environment for the deaf child to develop his or her skills and thrive through language acquisition.

In the United States, there are three main options available that incorporate the use of sign language in various degrees: residential schools, mainstream schools, and day schools for deaf children. Currently, mainstream schools are the most popular, but that does not mean that they are the best possible choice for all deaf children. Each option has advantages as well as disadvantages.

Sign On

A comprehensive listing of residential and day schools for deaf children in each of the 50 states can be found on the web at www.deaflibrary.org.

In the mid-1970s, laws were passed to give deaf children with special needs "equal and appropriate" education opportunities within public schools. Deaf education programs housed within public schools became known as mainstream schools. Children attend school during the day in Deaf-education classrooms. Depending on the school's program, they may receive an education combining speaking and signing English, signing in ASL, speechreading, or using oral methods. Mainstream schools tend to have more of an auditory focus than with residential or day schools. In many cases, parents of mainstreamed deaf children do not sign. These parents may hope that sending their child to these schools will help the child to learn how to communicate with the parents verbally. Sadly, in these cases a child may experience difficulty with English.

Residential schools, also known as "state schools," are similar to boarding schools. Children live in a dorm on campus away from their families. Some children may come home once a month or less. However, advantages are that they have a great opportunity to acquire language, as ASL is used as a primary communication method. They learn about Deaf culture and may get involved in many after-school activities. Many in the Deaf community believe that children who attend these schools are more apt to grow up to be confident and successful.

Day schools combine aspects of mainstream and residential schools. They are schools specifically for deaf children. Here, children can obtain the language and culture experience found in residential schools. Similar to a mainstream school, they can go home at night. Day schools have been successful in areas where they have been established. However, they are not widespread in the United States since many areas do not have a large enough population of deaf children or sufficient funding.

Sign Post

In a 1997 publication from Gallaudet University, researcher Edna Johnston conducted a study of mainstreaming schools versus residential schools across the Midwest. In the residential school environment, she found 43 percent of teachers were deaf, and all used ASL in the classrooms. Two thirds of students reported that they are "happy to be deaf." In contrast, mainstream programs reported 20 percent of their teachers were deaf, and less than one third of the programs include American Sign Language in their instruction. Half reported that they were "happy to be deaf."

What About College?

Advanced education is also highly possible and desirable for deaf people. With both under-graduate and graduate programs, Gallaudet University, located in Washington, D.C., is the only liberal arts university for deaf and hard-of-hearing students in the world. Gallaudet brings together deaf, hard-of-hearing, and hearing students as well as faculty in the common pursuit of education. It is a bilingual community in which both American Sign Language and English coexist and thrive.

Established in 1864, it remains the top authority in providing research and instruction on deaf-related studies. Every year, students graduate from Gallaudet University and go on to become doctors, lawyers, accountants, teachers, botanists—whatever they want to be.

Sign Post

Abraham Lincoln signed the charter authorizing the conferring of college degrees by the Columbia Institution for the Instruction of the Deaf and Dumb and the Blind, which eventually became named Gallaudet University.

Gallaudet is more than just a college to the Deaf community at large. It is a leader in the field of deafness, and is held in high regard. Gallaudet promotes programs that give confidence and dignity to those who are deaf. The Gallaudet community live by the tenets it explicitly states in its "Commitment to Sign Communication":

♦ We have the right and responsibility to understand and be understood. Clear and well-paced visual communication is a requirement for this learning community.

♦ We will respect the sign-language style of every individual and use whatever is necessary to communicate in a given situation.

♦ We will be assertive and sincere in our efforts to attain sign-language proficiency so we can communicate directly with each other.

♦ There is no linguistic minority at Gallaudet. Every member of the Gallaudet community enjoys the respect and the commitment to sign of everyone else.

On March 6–13, 1988, a significant event in Deaf history took place at Gallaudet University. Out of three final candidates, the Board of Trustees had elected Elisabeth Zinser to become President of the University. Unlike the other two candidates, she was hearing and had little to no knowledge of deafness or sign language. Staff, faculty, students, and the Deaf community were outraged. A revolution occurred among the students who protested "Deaf President Now."

The University was forced to close, and students blocked the entrances by holding signs that said "Deaf President Now." They protested for a week. Some camped out on the President's lawn. Others were present at a sit-in at the Mayflower Hotel, which was where the board was meeting to discuss the presidency. Still others held a protest march to Capitol Hill.

The students and their backers then presented the Board of Trustees with four demands:

◆ Elisabeth Zinser must resign and a deaf person selected president.

◆ Jane Spilman must step down as chairperson of the Board of Trustees.

◆ Deaf people must constitute a 51 percent majority on the Board.

◆ There would be no reprisals against any student or employee involved in the protest.

By the end of the week, the students' demands had been met and they ended their protest and proclaimed victory. Dr. I. King Jordan was named Gallaudet's eighth—and first—deaf president. Since 1864 the University had never had a deaf President, and now they had one. It was a proud and historic moment for the Deaf community as well as for Gallaudet University and its students. Out of this movement, the rest of the world heard the Deaf voice.

Other well-known colleges in America include the National Technical Institute for the Deaf part of the Rochester Institute of Technology) and the Southwest Collegiate institute for the Deaf (located in Big Spring, Texas).

What Should I Know so I Don't "Offend" a Deaf Person?

There are ways to be "politically correct" when referring to a deaf person. Deaf people want and deserve to have a nondegrading classification and words used to describe them. They don't label themselves as "handicapped" or "disabled." They are "handy capable" and "visually enabled" to do things. Deafness is not a disability; rather, it's a different way of being.

Sign On _____

Use these terms: deaf and hard-of hearing.

Sign Off _____

Don't say hearing-impaired, deaf and dumb, or deaf-mute.

What "Can" and "Can't" They Do?

Deaf people don't like the word "can't." The number of things that deaf people _can't do_ is limited. The number of things that they _can do_ is nearly unlimited!

They can go to college. They can shop. They can fly planes. They can build houses. They can read. They can write. They can give presentations. They can talk. They can act in movies. They can work and become productive members of tax-paying society. And, they can hold high-paying jobs as scientists, doctors, lawyers, accountants, actors, professors, engineers, bankers, and many more! They can do anything except in the areas that solely require the use of auditory means—such as work as a switchboard operator.

Sign Post

In 1990, Congress enacted the Americans with Disabilities Act (ADA) to establish a clear and comprehensive prohibition of discrimination on the basis of disability in employment, state, and local government, public accommodations, commercial facilities, transportation, and telecommunications. An individual with a disability is defined by the ADA as a person who has a physical or mental impairment that substantially limits one or more major life activities, a person who has a history or record of such an impairment, or a person who is perceived by others as having such an impairment. Applicable to employers of 15 people or more, the ADA prevents workplace discrimination on the basis of a disability and seeks for "equal opportunity" in the workplace.

They can even enjoy music. By feeling vibrations emitted from music, they can dance. Deaf people have an acute sense of vibrations, much more so than hearing people. Vibrations are felt through the body, particularly through hands (fingertips) and feet. In November 2001,

Dr. Dean Shibata, an assistant professor of radiology at the University of Washington, released the results of a study he conducted, which found that deaf people's brains rewire themselves so that they can "hear" vibrations given the absence of sound.

Sign Post

On September 17, 1994, 40 million television viewers of the Miss America pageant watched as Heather Whitestone—a deaf woman and accomplished ballerina—performed a beautiful dance performance perfectly set to the music. She won the pageant, the first-ever deaf woman to be crowned Miss America.

With the use of functional magnetic resonance imaging (fMRI), Dr. Shibata was able to compare the use of brain activity of deaf and hearing people as they had intermittent vibrations applied to their hands. While both deaf and hearing people showed brain activity associated with detecting hand vibrations and the sense of touch, deaf people showed additional brain activity from the stimulation. Dr. Shibata found that the auditory complex—the part of the brain used by hearing people to process sound for hearing—is also used by deaf people to process vibrations for feeling. In this way, deaf people use the "hearing" part of the brain to "listen" to vibrations. Dr. Shibata suggests that his findings make a strong case for exposing deaf children to music early in life; such exposure would help the auditory cortex of the brain to develop and maximize their chances of enjoying music.

Sign On

At the release of Dr. Shibata's study, Dr. John Low, the Director of Technology at the Royal National Institute for Deaf People said: "The enjoyment of music by deaf people has been overlooked too long, and the findings appear to support the experiences reported by deaf people."

Deaf people can even compose music! Ludwig van Beethoven, one of the greatest classical musical composers, became deaf at the age of 28. He relied on sound vibrations to help him "hear" the music. For the next 10 years, he went on to compose some of his most famous works, none of which he ever heard with his own ears.

Sign Post

From 1802 to 1812, Beethoven completed Symphony 2,3; Eroica, 4, 5, 6; Pastoral, 7 and 8; Piano Concerto no. 4 and no. 5; Emperor; The Violin Concerto; Opera, Fidellio; The Three Rasumovski String Quartets; and a wealth of piano sonatas and other works.

Can Deaf People Drive Cars?

In the United States, there are few restrictions on deaf people obtaining a license to drive. However, in certain states (such as New Jersey and Illinois) deaf drivers may have a code ("J88") on their licenses to indicate that they are deaf. Some other states (such as Florida and Oregon) require that they may be required to have an outside rearview mirror mounted on the left side of the vehicle or to wear a hearing aid. Some deaf people may choose to have modifications added to their cars, such as multilight panels added to dashboards to warn them of emergency vehicles nearby. These devices can rate the type of sound and can distinguish whether the sound is emitted from a wailing ambulance siren or a blaring car horn.

But many deaf drivers do not use assistive devices while driving, and rely heavily upon their keen visual abilities. Because driving is primarily a visual activity, deaf drivers often excel. It may surprise hearing people to learn that deaf drivers have a better overall safety record than their hearing counterparts do. Hearing people have more distractions while they are on the roads—think of all accidents caused by using cell phones or adjusting the volume or changing stations on car radios.

Sign On

Charging deaf people more for automobile insurance is an old injustice. Nowadays, they do not have to pay an extra fee in their premiums.

Not all countries permit deaf people to drive. According to statistics from the World Federation of the Deaf (WFD), at least 26 countries (such as India and China) do not allow deaf citizens to hold a driver's license.

Can a Deaf Person Communicate Using a Telephone?

Absolutely! Deaf people can "talk" to members of the Deaf community as well as with hearing people.

Deaf people communicate with each other on the telephone through the use of a teletypewriter device called a TTY (abbreviated from the phrase Telephone Teletypes). The TTY looks like a mini typewriter with a display screen, or a simple word processor. It is equipped with acoustic cups or direct connect modes that are turned on when a call comes in. TTYs enable a person to type text messages emitted via the telephone line to be received by another TTY user. In this way, they can type messages back and forth to one another.

Sign On _____

As TTYs become more widespread in public places (such as in libraries, hotels, airports, and public phone booths), you may see signs posted for "TDD." TDD stands for Telecommunication Device for the Deaf.

TTYs have come a long way since they were first developed in the mid-1960s. Once enormous and bulky (some stood three feet high), they are now made to be either large to comfortably sit on a table or desk, or small enough to be portable in fit in a jacket pocket.

Sign Post _____

Alexander Graham Bell, the inventor of the telephone, had great ties to the Deaf community. His mother was hard-of-hearing. He married a deaf woman. He invented microphones to help deaf people hear speech better. Additionally, he taught deaf students at schools for the deaf in Boston and London.

If a hearing person doesn't have a TTY, he or she can still communicate with a deaf person on the phone through the use of a Relay Center. To do this, a hearing person first calls the Relay Center Communications Assistant directly and gives the phone number of a deaf person. The Communications Assistant then dials the number and connects to the deaf person's TTY. Once connected, the TTY user types a message to the Communications Assistant who "relays" it by reading the typed message aloud to the hearing person. The Communications Assistant then listens to the hearing person's reply and relays it back to the TTY user through type.

Relay calls are also possible without a TTY! In addition to this standard phone TTY service, many Relay Centers also have an Internet relay service that allows calls to be typed over a web-enabled computer. Additionally, some may offer a video relay service that uses sign-language interpreters, a web camera, and high-speed Internet connection to serve relay users who prefer to communicate in real time in sign language.

Sign On _____

In relay conversations, the abbreviations GA and SK are used. GA means GO-AHEAD and is used when one is finished with a message and is ready to signal the other person to go ahead with his or her message. SK means STOP KEYING and is used to close and end the call.

How does a deaf person know when he or she is receiving a call? A device called a visual ring signaler is hooked up to the telephone and a lamp (most often, multiple lamps are used). When the phone rings, the visual ring signaler flashes the lamp to blink on and off to bring attention to an incoming call. The visual ring signaler may also be hooked up to a doorbell, so that when someone rings the bell the light will again flash on and off. Another device, a baby-cry signaler, works in the same way and can be used to detect a cry in the baby's room and signal it to a lamp in the parent's room.

With all this light flashing, how does a deaf person know if it's a telephone call, doorbell, or baby's cry? The devices allow for blinking variations, such as having a telephone call signal flash light on and off very fast, and a doorbell flash on and off in a short rhythmic pattern.

Other technology commonly used for communication include FAX machines, pagers (deaf people keep it on the vibrate mode), and Internet e-mail and instant-messenger web services.

There are even website chat rooms that are designed to be a place for deaf, hard-of-hearing, and hearing people of all ages to discuss Deaf issues, world events, jokes, and to join in friendly and fun conversation.

Sign On _____

While technology has allowed for alternative communications, the most preferred way to communicate is face-to-face.

What's next in phone technology? Deaf people may be able to use cell phones soon, too. A consortium of researchers from Germany, Sweden, Spain, and the United Kingdom are working together on a project called Wireless Information Services for Deaf People on the Move (WISDOM). The researchers are devising a way to incorporate sign language recognition technology into third-generation (3G) cellular phones. With this technology, deaf users will be able to call up news, weather, and sports information in sign language from a video server via 3G phones, give commands to their phones in sign language, and access a real-time interpretation service to communicate with hearing people. In laboratory conditions, it is reported that the technology can already understand sentences having as many as nine signs in them with a recognition rate of 90 percent.

Can Deaf People Watch Television?

Closed captioning makes it possible to understand dialogues and sounds on the television. Closed captioning is embedded in the television signal and becomes visible when you use a closed captioned feature. The viewers see captions on the television screen (usually at the bottom), similar to the experience of watching subtitles in a foreign film. Closed captioning reflects what is being said or heard on television programs. For example, on a comedy show, when there is no dialogue but there is laughter heard, the caption will read "audience laughing."

Most shows (and commercials!) have closed captioning nowadays. After a show is taped, caption writers use scripts and listen to a show's soundtrack so that they can add words that explain sound effects. Some older programs that were produced before captioning became widespread have added captions for their syndicated reruns.

Sign Post _____

Not only is closed captioning used by deaf people, it is also extremely helpful to people learning English or learning to read. It is also helpful in noisy environments such as in an airport terminal, health club, or restaurant/sports bar.

Sometimes programs are captioned in real time. Generally this happens during a live broadcast of a special event or of an important news program. There is a delay of a few seconds before a stenographer can enter the captions into a special computer program to show what is being said. This service is particularly valuable during times of newsworthy emergencies.

Additionally, many movie VHS cassettes and most DVDs have the option for closed caption so that deaf people can watch movies right from their television, too. They are marked with a label coded "cc" embedded in a box found on the cover of the VHS or DVD.

Sign On _____

Chances are that your television has closed captioning! A law in the United States called the "Television Decoder Circuitry Act of 1990" mandates that since July 1993, all televisions manufactured for sale in the U.S. must contain a built-in caption decoder if the picture tube is 13 inches or larger. Check your manual for instructions on how to enable it, so that you can experience this, too!

The Least You Need to Know

◆ Deaf children can go to all-deaf residential or day schools, or may choose to be mainstreamed into Deaf education programs in public schools.

◆ Use the terms deaf and hard-of hearing. Don't say hearing-impaired, deaf and dumb, or deaf-mute.

◆ The number of things that deaf people *can't do* is limited. The number of things that they *can do* is unlimited!

◆ Deaf people can do many of the same things that hearing people can do: work, enjoy music, drive, go to the movies, use a telephone, watch television.

◆ Relay Centers make it possible for hearing people (who don't have a TTY) to call a deaf person on the phone or via the Internet.

◆ Gallaudet is the largest Deaf liberal arts college in the world, and has both undergraduate and graduate programs. Its research institute serves as a top authority in the area of Deaf-related studies.

In This Chapter

- ◆ Variations of sign language in America
- ◆ Signing around the globe
- ◆ Common misconceptions and true facts
- ◆ Benefits for you and, surprise, babies, too!

Chapter 3

Understanding the "Signed" Language

From an early age we're taught to communicate with our voices. Whether we speak English, French, Japanese, or any other language, it's all about the sounds and words we form coming from our mouths to other peoples' ears. But we have other body parts that are just waiting to be used! Our hands, faces, and bodies can all be utilized to create messages and express thoughts, feelings, and actions. Sign language, being visual in nature, helps us to convey meanings in ways we may have never been able to before! Look at your hands and consider the power you hold in it. Your fingers can be the source of communicating a message that can brighten a deaf person's day or help them with a problem or issue she faces.

In this chapter we explore the language of sign, its variations in America and across the world, and put to rest some common misconceptions about its use. You'll learn about how it can benefit your life as a hearing person with existing language skills, and also the life of a baby just beginning to acquire language.

What Is Sign Language?

Sign Language is a unique, living language that is fun to learn. You will find that it challenges you in ways that no auditory language will. It will require you to use your hands, face, and body to express yourself—not your voice. By signing, you'll be communicating in a way so that others can visually understand you—whether you're delivering a complex message or asking a simple question.

Sign On

Sign language is a generic term for many forms of manual communication.

There are several major variations of sign language used by deaf people. According to their education and cultural values, deaf people will prefer to use one or more variations.

Sign Post

Most members of the Deaf Community in the United States use American Sign Language and are bilingual (with English as their second language).

American Sign Language (ASL) is considered to be its own language. Borrowing from ASL are Signed English (SE) and Contact Signing (CS). CS is formerly known as Pidgin Signed English (PSE). CS can vary in its usage and sometimes appears to be more ASL-like, while at other times more English-like. CS is the most used communication method between deaf signers and hearing signers. It is widely used in social activities where both deaf and hearing people come together to socialize or converse in informal or casual settings.

Sign On

ASL is the third most-used language in the United States; the first is English and the second is Spanish.

There is a controversy due to differing philosophies of how sign language should be taught. Some feel very strongly about teaching ASL and only ASL as the language to be used with deaf people. Again, this is because ASL is the primary language within the Deaf community. At the opposite extreme, some feel strongly about teaching SE, because English is the primary language in this country. This issue is continually being debated among deaf and hearing signers as well as in the deaf education field at large.

Years of experience and research indicate that sign language used between deaf and hearing people actually combines elements from both ASL and SE. This mode of communication is called Contact Signing. With CS, some sign-language users tend to be more ASL-like, while others tend to be more SE-like in use of grammar and syntax. This flexibility is influenced by one's education of ASL and/or SE.

SE uses English sentence structure, adding additional signs to express components of English grammar. As a communication mode, Contact Signing (CS) falls somewhere in the middle between SE and ASL. CS preserves the conceptual meaning of ASL while using varied degrees of English word order and ASL sign order. It is a highly flexible and useful communication form that serves the purpose of bridging the gap between deaf and hearing people when they are together. We take a further in-depth look at these visual communication variations now.

American Sign Language (ASL)

ASL is a free-flowing, complex, visual-spatial language that is unique unto itself. ASL is made up of signs created with the hands, facial expressions, and body posture and movement. It conveys ideas, information, and emotion with as much range, complexity, and versatility as spoken languages. ASL uses the physical space in front of a signer to create visual concepts. Facial expressions and body language are very important here; ASL communication depends on expression and facial grammar with ASL mouth movements. ASL does not share any grammatical similarities to English, and it should not it be considered a broken, mimed, or gestured form of English.

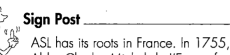

Sign Post

ASL has its roots in France. In 1755, Abbe Charles Michel de L'Epee of Paris established the first free school for deaf people. Having studied a group of deaf people and how they communicated with each other, he realized that there could be a defined sign used to suggest a desired concept. The Abbe went on to put together a language system that combined conventional gestures, hand signs, and fingerspelling to help express full thoughts. He paved the way for deaf people to have a more standardized language of their own and taught them how to communicate with themselves and the hearing world through a more formal language system.

Many deaf people use American Sign Language (ASL) when speaking with others within the Deaf community in the United States and some parts of Canada. ASL is the standard language of deaf people, as well as for hearing children born into deaf families. Some hearing people who have advanced sign skills and great knowledge of Deaf culture learn ASL as well (many of these people are professional Sign Language interpreters and/or teachers).

Sign On

ASL studies are promoted before one enters a formal Interpreter Education Program.

ASL has developed over time within the Deaf community, just as spoken English has been developed within the hearing community. ASL seeks to convey a concept. ASL signs express meanings, *not* English words. To further explain, ASL signs express "meanings of concepts visually" whereas English words express "meanings of concepts auditorily."

Sign Post

There was an ideological conflict between French deaf teacher Thomas Gallaudet and the American researcher, Alexander Graham Bell. Bell believed that it was best to teach deaf children how to read lips and speak in English. Gallaudet believed that it was best to teach deaf children a language that they could fully participate in, and he later created the modern version of ASL that is used today.

ASL has its own syntax and grammar. Because its sentence structure is so different from spoken English, deaf people tend to experience difficulty writing complete sentences, which requires the utilization of tense, articles, conjunctions, and prepositions.

So what's ASL syntax structure?

Time tense + topic/subject + color + any other adjectives + action

ASL is not a written language, but to illustrate ASL syntax structure for you, the following are some examples of what ASL "sentences" would look like if you were to write them out—that is, the words you would use and the way you would sign the words.

◆ TODAY CAR SMALL BLUE ME DRIVE (English: I'm driving a small blue car today.)
◆ LATER EVENING MOVIE ME GO (English: I will go to the movie later this evening.)
◆ LONG-AGO TELEPHONE NONE (English: A long time ago we did not have a telephone.)
◆ PAST CHILDREN SWIM (English: The children went swimming.)
◆ TWO-YEAR-AGO COAT BLACK WHITE ME BUY (English: I bought a black and white coat two years ago.)

Sign On _____

With regards to syntax, ASL is closer to spoken Japanese than to English.

Signed English (SE)

Signed English expands upon signs used in ASL by adding prefixes, tenses, and endings to give a clear and complete visual presentation of English.

SE is an English-based sign system that matches the elements of spoken English—every word, word-ending, and prefix is signed. Given this, more signing time is required. Because it takes more concentration and focus to sign every word and word prefix or ending, less emphasis is on facial expression or body language. There is a greater emphasis on speechreading in order to fully experience the English word.

Using SE is a topic of controversy. Some schools use SE when teaching deaf children because they believe that it accurately and completely conveys the English language well and facilitates reading (which has been a common issue for deaf adults). Conversely, there are studies that show that SE, due to its inability to conceptually translate information, may be detrimental to acquiring literacy.

Sign Off _____

Many deaf people express their frustration with users of SE because it takes a longer time to communicate using it and because it is so different from ASL (their natural, native language).

So what's it like to sign in SE?

Again, for illustrative purposes only, here are some examples of what SE "sentences" would look like if you were to write them out—the words you would use and the way you would sign the words.

◆ I AM DRIVE + ING A SMALL BLUE CAR TODAY (English: I'm driving a small blue car today.)

◆ I WILL GO TO THE MOVIE LATER THIS EVENING (English: I will go to the movie later this evening.)

◆ A LONG TIME AGO WE D-I-D NOT HAVE A TELEPHONE (English: A long time ago we did not have a telephone.)

◆ THE CHILDREN GO + PAST SWIM + ING (English: The children went swimming.)

◆ I BUY + PAST A BLACK AND WHITE COAT TWO YEAR AGO (English: I bought a black and white coat two years ago.)

Contact Signing (CS)

Generally speaking, a contact system develops over time as two different language speakers make "contact" with each other. In this case, as hearing people (who use English) and deaf people (those who use ASL) made contact with one another, a form of communication began to develop that used parts of both English and ASL. This is now called Contact Signing.

Deaf people naturally use ASL among themselves. Hearing people may use English among themselves. It is interesting to observe social interactions between hearing and deaf people trying to communicate in sign. The reality is, when a signed conversation is observed between deaf and hearing, deaf people tend to switch from using ASL to CS and hearing people switch from speaking English to using CS. They make an unspoken compromise and, among themselves, assess each other's vocabulary/grammar level, and then use a signed communication mode that is clear to both parties.

Contact Signing is the most widely used communication mode in the United States among deaf and hearing persons. CS is also referred to as "conversational sign language," and is the mode that we will use when teaching sign phrases in this book.

For some hearing people who wish to pursue their studies and careers in deafness such as interpretation and/or teacher education, it is highly recommended that American Sign Language be the focus of their study (and we recommend that they should learn it via college courses). For the majority of hearing people who wish to communicate in sign language for basic conversations with deaf people, CS is the most used and preferred form between hearing and deaf signers.

Sign On

Contact Signing continues to grow in popularity and is widely used by both deaf and hearing people.

CS incorporates ASL signs in somewhat English word order. Signs are used with an attempt to retain the conceptual meaning of ASL rather than English. CS vocabulary is drawn from ASL. Words that do not "carry information" (e.g., to, the, am) are often not used, and nor are the word endings of English (e.g., -ed, -s, -ment) added to signs.

So what's it like to sign in Contact Signing? Just as we showed you above for illustrative purposes only, the following are some examples of what CS "sentences" would look like if you were to write them out—the words you would use and the way you would sign the words:

◆ ME DRIVE SMALL BLUE CAR TODAY (English: I'm driving a small blue car today.)
◆ ME GO MOVIE LATER EVENING (English: I will go to the movie later this evening.)
◆ LONG-AGO WE NO-HAVE TELE-PHONE (English: A long time ago we did not have a telephone.)
◆ CHILDREN SWIM FINISH (English: The children went swimming.)
◆ ME BUY BLACK WHITE COAT TWO-YEAR-AGO (English: I bought a black and white coat two years ago.)

Sign Post

Again, the goal of this book is to encourage deaf and hearing people to communicate conversationally with each other. Based on our life experience and research, this book will indicate typical conversations between deaf and hearing people across America using Contact Signing.

Common Misconceptions

Because its purpose and meaning are not widely understood by hearing people, there are some views out there on sign language that are not entirely accurate. Here are a few examples:

Misconception	Fact
Signs are a form of fingerspelling.	Signs are separate from fingerspelling, in which a hand configuration is used to represent a letter of the English alphabet. Fingerspelling can be a part of a signed dialogue, when needed to communicate an English term or name.
ASL is iconic/pictorial and is a form of pantomime.	Pantomime is not a language; it uses generic motions and gestures to communicate. It is a continuous movement with no well-defined transitions. ASL is a language, having its own defined grammar rules, discrete handshapes, locations, distinct movements, orientations, and transitions.
ASL can only be used to carry on simple and short dialogues.	ASL includes signs capable for discussing complex, in-depth, or abstract thoughts and ideas. ASL is used in lengthy conversations, professional discourse, and lectures, just like any other language is used.
ASL has a sign for every English word.	Although there are hundreds of thousands of English words, there are fewer than 10,000 signs in ASL dictionaries (Random House Webster's American Sign Language Dictionary has 5,600 signs, and the unabridged American Sign Language Dictionary by Martin Sternberg has just over 7,000 entries), although new signs are continually being developed and added (just as new words are continually added to English). In ASL, some English words are signed the same way—e.g., bird and chicken are both represented by using the same sign and the context clarifies its meaning.
ASL signs are universal and the same around the world.	ASL is only one of many sign languages found around the world. ASL is mainly used within the Deaf community in the United States and also in English-speaking parts of Canada.

Sign Post

There aren't signs for every English word (just as there aren't English words for every sign). While the most comprehensive sign-language dictionaries have fewer than 10,000 signs, the Oxford English Dictionary released in December, 2003, defines over 500,000 words. That said, about 200,000 words are in common use today, and an educated person has a vocabulary of about 20,000 words.

If there is no sign for an English word you're trying to express, then it's preferred for you to use gestures. Fingerspelling is another option.

Signing Around the World

Just as there are different variations of languages spoken around the world (e.g., English, Spanish, Italian, French, Chinese, Japanese, Portuguese, Hindi), there also are different sign languages around the world. It is also common for sign languages to reflect regional or local "dialects." Why? Because signs are developed within Deaf communities in every country, some of the things they do, use, or think may be different.

Think of a telephone. The telephone itself has changed over the years, and signs have evolved to more accurately capture this changing device. And depending on where one lives in the world, the sign for telephone will reflect the system most often used in his or her region. Years ago, Americans may have signed PHONE with one hand visually illustrating holding the receiver to the head, and another hand imitating the action of dialing up a number. This sign changed when we had touch-tone phone systems; one hand would look as if it held the receiver to the head, and another hand imitated the action of pressing keys on the touch-pad. Today, some sign PHONE to reflect cell phones—one hand looks as if it is flipping open the top of the phone and holding it close to the head.

Sign Post

The Ethnologue Index lists 103 sign languages used by deaf people around the world. Like any other language, a sign language requires a population to actively develop, use, and maintain it. However, in many societies, deaf people live in communities where there may not be a critical mass of other signers needed to sustain a true sign language. Therefore, what happens is that each deaf person develops an agreed contact-signing system to use with his or her relatives and neighbors.

Sign Post

The following are some examples of sign languages in use around the world today:

◆ American Sign Language (ASL)
◆ Spanish Sign Language (LSE)
◆ Auslan, used in Australia
◆ Kenya Sign Language (KSL)
◆ British Sign Language (BSL)
◆ Dutch Sign Language (NGT)
◆ French Sign Language (LSF)
◆ Irish Sign Language (ISL)
◆ Nicaraguan Sign Language (LSN)
◆ Taiwanese Sign Language (TSL)

Why isn't there an international sign language? Think of how the spoken language, Esperanto, was introduced as a new universal spoken language in the late nineteenth century. Esperanto does not belong to any country or ethnic group: It is a neutral, international language. It was hoped that it would form a worldwide community so that people from all over the world could come together and have a common language to speak together. But Esperanto didn't really catch on. Esperanto is not commonly used, and many people still don't know about it. By contrast, English has gained in popularity around the world, and is even required as a second language for schoolchildren in many foreign countries.

Just as an international spoken language was developed and tried, the same holds true for an international sign language. The concept of an international sign language was discussed by the World Congress of the World Federation of the Deaf in 1951. Years later, in 1973, a committee tried to invent a universal sign language. This language was called Gestuno, which is roughly translated to mean "the unity of sign languages" in Italian. The committee published a book with about 1500 signs, and they had tried to choose the most understandable signs from diverse sign languages to make Gestuno easy to learn. However, Gestuno is SEnas a system of gestures and does not have a concrete grammar, so some believe that it is not a language.

Sign On _____

In recent years, a growing number of states have passed legislation to recognize American Sign Language (ASL) as a foreign language and to permit high schools and universities to accept it in fulfillment of foreign language requirements. By July 1997, 28 states had passed this legislation, and several colleges and universities (including the University of California system, Massachusetts Institute of Technology, Brown University, Georgetown University, and the University of Washington) accept ASL as a foreign language for academic or elective credit.

Why You May Want to Learn ASL

Why should you learn sign language? Surely one reason is for social purposes. Deaf people out there—they could be your family, friends, neighbors, and co-workers—would love to communicate with you and share their joys, sorrows, dreams, ambitions, love, hopes, and lives. And it is highly useful to know sign language in times of emergency for deaf people who are in a crisis and need aid. Don't forget about the fact that you'll be able to help deaf people who need assistance with directions, or to give them an explanation of what's going on around them that they can't hear.

Some people go on to work as sign-language interpreters as a part-time or full-time career. Sign-language interpreters provide services for both deaf and hearing people in courts, medical appointments, banks, job interviews, theaters, places of worship, and classrooms. The demand for qualified sign-language interpreters has risen dramatically over the last 10 years in the business world, in the creative and performing arts, in computer and telecommunications

industries, and particularly in education. Many states require that all sign-language interpreters have certification from either the Registry of Interpreters for the Deaf (RID) or the National Association of the Deaf (NAD). Others require that sign-language interpreters have an Associate's Degree from an approved interpreter-education program.

Sign Post _____

Top-10 reasons for learning sign language ...

1. It's a beautiful, fun, and lively language.
2. You can talk to someone on the other side of a window.
3. You can chat underwater.
4. You can acquire fluency in another language (and perhaps be bilingual or multilingual).
5. You can talk and talk as much as you like in a quiet setting, such as a library.
6. You can carry a conversation in a noisy setting (such as in a bar).
7. You can talk with deaf people.
8. You can secretly communicate a message about something (or someone!) without other people overhearing you.
9. You can talk to someone across the street.
10. You can sign with your mouth full.

Babies Can Learn Sign Language, Too!

Teaching signs to a newborn has been done for centuries by deaf parents with their deaf or hearing babies. However, there is a new concept for hearing parents to teach hearing babies how to sign.

It is a natural inclination for babies to use their hands for visual communication and gesturing. For example, without being taught, they may lift their hands to their mouth as if to communicate EAT or DRINK. Babies may use their fingers and hands to point to something that they want or like. Additionally, a baby may reach out her arms to communicate that she wishes to be picked up or carried. Clearly, teaching a baby sign language capitalizes on her natural tendencies for gesturing.

Sign On

Babies who sign ...
- ◆ Speak earlier than nonsigners
- ◆ Experience less frustration
- ◆ Develop larger vocabularies
- ◆ Become better readers
- ◆ Have IQs that are at least 10–12 points higher

Research studies show many benefits of babies (particularly newborns) who learn how to sign. Before babies have control over their voices, they have control over their hands and thus can sign at an earlier age than they can speak. So, babies who sign may be less frustrated since they have a way of expressing their wants and needs. Meaning, they may cry less, as their needs are being satisfied. Additionally, it has been reported that babies can sign in simple sentences by the time they reach the age of 10 months—this ability to converse is much ahead of a child who only communicates with his voice.

Research also shows babies who are taught a few simple signs speak earlier than nonsigners, and also have larger vocabularies and become better readers. This is because more synapses of their brains are stimulated and this allows for rapid and expanded learning.

Sign Post

Baby Fingers, a company based in New York City and founded by Lori Heller, provides sign-language instruction through songs to parents and their babies aged one month to five years. Lori and her staff teach signs through music, which research has proven to enhance language development, spatial reasoning skills, socialization, and motivation to communicate. Baby Fingers states that as both signing and music are rhythmic, the combination aids in the ability to keep a steady beat; this skill has been linked to improved reading performance.

The Least You Need to Know

- ◆ Sign language is a living language that changes within cultures over time.
- ◆ Sign language is the third most-used language in the United States.
- ◆ ASL is most commonly used among deaf people; CS is most commonly used when a deaf person and a hearing person engage in conversation.
- ◆ Sign Language is not universal—It is different in each country and even has regional or local variations.
- ◆ Some people learn sign language for social purposes, while others learn it for professional reasons.
- ◆ Babies who learn sign language have an advantage in language development over those who don't.

In This Part

Part

Getting Ready to Sign—
Express Yourself!

In this part, we prepare you for learning signs and communicating visually. It is a physical language—one that requires the use of your hands, face, and body. You don't just communicate a message solely with your hands! There's a lot to know about how to make use of your body parts as well as the space around you.

In This Chapter

- ◆ Using your senses other than "hearing"
- ◆ Setting the stage for communicating with a deaf person
- ◆ Using your voice when signing
- ◆ Having an appropriate attire and appearance

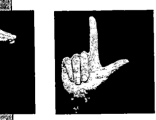

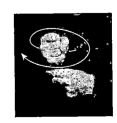

Signing Etiquette

Being deaf is an "invisible" way of being. Unlike blindness or paralysis, which are immediately visible when you look at someone with dark glasses carrying a cane or sitting in a wheelchair, deaf people look just the same as hearing people. Given a photograph, it would be tough to tell who the deaf person was unless he or she was wearing an obvious hearing-assisted device. Because of this, hearing people may be surprised or taken aback when they first discover a person next to them is deaf, because it is unexpected. Hearing people may then become fearful, intimidated, or shy because they don't know how to make themselves understood in a conversation with a deaf person.

This chapter aims to break down the communication barrier. It will expose you to the things you should do, should not do, and what you should wear (yes, we did just say this!) to communicate effectively with a deaf person.

"Sensing" a Message

As a hearing person talking to another hearing person, you may just speak and rely on the fact that sound will travel from your lips to the ears of another person. But, what is it that you need to do to be sure that the hearing person receives your message?

◆ Have enough volume so they can hear you, for sure, and adjust the volume in your voice based on the level of background noise. If there's music playing from the radio, speak louder so that the person can hear your voice above it. The same goes if you're trying to yell at someone who's in the kitchen to get you a can of soda when you're comfortably sitting far away in the living room.

◆ Speak clearly, don't mumble. You try to make sure that you say things that will prevent the other person from having to ask you, "What was that again? I didn't catch what you said."

So, volume and clarity are key for the delivery and receipt of a message between two hearing people. Just as you have to be aware of things that distract your communication with another hearing person, you need to be aware of things that could be distracting when you communicate with a deaf person.

Because deaf people don't take in information primarily through their ears, they rely on many of their other senses to receive messages. Sight, smell, touch, feel—these senses are all heightened to a deaf person since they don't use the sense of hearing. They'll primarily be looking at your face and lips, and watching your body language, too.

Simple Guidelines of Communication

Seeing with one's eyes can be quite a multi-tasking experience. Remember that a deaf person has to take in a great amount of visual information from their natural environment, physical surroundings, and people passing by, and from their signing partner's eye contact, facial expressions, head tilting and shaking, and body movements and signs. There's a lot of "visual noise" out there! So how can you make sure you're setting the stage for good communication with a deaf person?

Things to make sure you're doing (and not doing) include the following:

◆ Turn your face and body toward the person and look right at his or her face.

◆ Maintain eye contact for the duration of the conversation.

◆ Make sure that you have the person's attention before you begin the conversation.

Sign On _____

If a sign-language interpreter is present, continue to talk directly to the deaf person—do not speak directly to the interpreter. Depending on the deaf person's receptive skills, she will look at the interpreter and may glance at your face to see expressions, or speechread. Deaf people like to have face-to-face contact and the opportunity to receive the communication message from both of you and the interpreter simultaneously.

◆ Cut out background noise so that it is not distracting to someone wearing a hearing aid (including radios and televisions).

◆ Position yourself in good lighting ... a silhouette is difficult to understand.

◆ Stand at a distance of three to six feet.

◆ Get to the point and be direct with your communication message.

◆ Wait for your turn to start signing (the same etiquette as when speaking).

◆ Relax!

Sign Off _____

If you see other people sign, avoid watching their conversation unless you intend to introduce yourself.

It is important for you to have patience when communicating with a deaf person. Instead of getting frustrated and immediately thinking that he doesn't understand you, take some time to really focus on the person and the messages that are being shared. Reflect on the guidelines above and consider if there's something that you can do to facilitate a great conversation!

Should You Use Your Voice?

Here is another issue of controversy: Should you speak English and use signs at the same time? ASL educators and language scientists feel strongly that hearing people should not use their voice while signing as it may take away from the visual message. On the other hand, SE educators feel strongly that hearing people should use voice while signing as it adds another sense to the visual message.

Sign Post

Depending on how much speech training or education a deaf person had while learning how to speak, her speech may not be clear to a hearing person. Sometimes, words that are attempted to be spoken are received as unfamiliar sounds to a hearing person. Also, a deaf person may also not be aware of the volume of her voice (whether trying to speak, laugh, or cry).

While engaged in conversation, some deaf people may or may not use their voice, depending on their confidence or comfort level with how they think their voice sounds to a hearing person. Some hearing people may or may not use voice because they realize that the person they are communicating with can't hear them anyway. Yet, some hearing people may mouth words along with their signs because they want to ensure clarity, or just out of habit! Whether or not you use your voice or mouth words along with signs is a personal option, and may be discussed with the deaf person if you think it could aid to the delivery of your messages.

Getting Attention

To get another hearing person's attention you would generally shout at her or call to her—In other words, you increase the volume of your voice. But what if the other person can't hear you? How would you get her to pay attention to you or notice that you were trying to say something? To answer this question, keep in mind that deaf people are sensitive to movement as well as to vibrations.

Sign On

Deaf people are sensitive to light and movement. Their eyes quickly catch action and signals.

There are many different ways of getting deaf people's attention visually without ever having to use your voice, including the following:

◆ Tap lightly and gently on their shoulder and/or arm using the pads of your fingertips (but do not touch elsewhere on the body to get attention, such as the head, face, stomach).

Sign Off

Do not poke, tap, or slap hard. Do not tap the back of a deaf person or sneak up on him or her unexpectedly.

◆ Walk over and stand in their line of sight to make yourself seen.
◆ Wave gently at them—this could be from across a room or standing in front of them.
◆ Flicker the lights on and off once at a normal speed (flickering lights too slow or too fast, signals a deaf person to critical attention or emergency).

Sign On

If you need to call the attention of many deaf people in a room (e.g., to alert them that the place is closing for the night), it is customary to flick the lights twice. If people still do not pay attention, then flick twice again.

◆ Tap your foot firmly (but do not stomp) on the floor if vibrations can be felt.

Sign Post

Wooden floors allow for vibrations to be carried through. Concrete and marble do not allow for vibrations to be felt.

◆ Tap a table lightly (if the deaf person is sitting at the same table).
◆ Do not kick or throw things to get attention.

If you are outdoors in the dark, use a flashlight and wave to get a deaf person's attention. If you do not have a flashlight, use other light means such as lighting a match. You could also try waving in front of a lantern or a lamp.

It's What You Wear, Too!

Yes, the clothes you wear are an important factor, too. Deaf people have to look at your body language, facial expressions, lip movement, and hand signs; their eyes are working overtime just to get your message! It doesn't help if they're taking this all in against a background that has some "loud" action going on—meaning, you'll certainly make their eyes sore if you wear bright neon colors, pinstripes, dots, and such. It's just all too much to take in at once!

What kind of clothes should you wear? Clothes that provide contrasts to your skin color. Some guidelines for clothing colors and patterns include the following:

◆ Dark colors (e.g., black, navy blue, brown, grey, dark green, purple, deep red) for people who have light skin tones.
◆ Light colors (e.g., off-white, tan, peach, pink, light blue) for people with darker skin tones.
◆ Solid colored clothing (e.g., avoid patterns such as stripes, polka dots, or heavy plaids).

Sign Off

Anything close to your skin tone is a no-no. So, if you're Caucasian, that means no whites or off-whites. If you're darker-skinned, browns may be difficult. Look in the mirror to make sure you don't look too washed out, or you'll just fade out.

Sign On

A neutral color of polish may be worn, such as clear, light pink, or peach.

In Addition to Clothing ...

Besides your attire, your appearance matters, too. Remember, a deaf person is taking the "whole you" into their sight.

If you do wear jewelry, make sure that it is plain and not visually or tactfully distracting. Avoid wearing large, bulky, or very colorful rings, bracelets, and necklaces that may interrupt the flow of communication. Also avoid sparkling or dangling long earrings that may reflect light and cause interference.

Fingernails should look short, neat, and filed smooth. Rough edges can be irritating to look at, and rough to the touch. Nails that are too long are distracting for your communication partner, and may make it difficult for you to sign, too! Nail polish—such as bright reds, dark colors, and fancy decals or airbrushed designs—make it tough for a viewer to watch your fingers.

The Least You Need to Know

◆ Follow the Simple Guidelines for Communication so that you can have an effective setting for conversation.

◆ Using your voice or mouthing words along with signs is a personal option, and may be discussed with the deaf person if it could be helpful for better communication.

◆ Get a deaf person's attention by making use of her sensitivity to motion, light, movement, and vibrations.

◆ Wear clothes that contrast your skin color, and keep your jewelry and nail polish simple.

In This Chapter

◆ Using facial expressions

◆ Performing speechreading

◆ Using body language and body movements

◆ Signing within your "signing space"

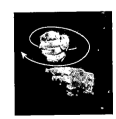

Chapter 5

Expressing Yourself!

All of us—hearing and deaf—observe and interpret other peoples' faces and body language. And we do this every day. We look into a woman's eyes when she says "I love you" or "I'm not lying" to judge her sincerity. If we see a man giving a big smile and hearty laugh that makes his shoulders shake, we think he is happy. If someone scrunches up her eyebrows, shakes her head, and stiffens her body, we think she is in disagreement. The face and body are wonderful, efficient instruments to communicate our emotions and reinforce the messages that we're delivering in a conversion.

In this chapter, we look at how we can use our faces, bodies, and the space immediately around us to express what we're feeling and thinking.

The Eyes Have It!

Hearing people frequently talk to each other without looking directly at the other person. A hearing person may continue talking when she is leaning down to pick something up, staring at a television or movie screen, reading a book, or even when turning around and walking away. It is considered normal and not necessary to look at another person 100 percent of the time when speaking to her.

Not so when you communicate with a deaf person! Eye contact is critical in getting your message across. Remember that sign language is a highly visual language. It is necessary to keep your eyes on the signer in order to actively engage in conversation.

Some hearing people become uncomfortable with a high level of eye contact; they perceive it as "staring." Deaf people don't see it this way (pun intended!). It is common for deaf people to steadily look at another person to let her know that they would like to begin a discussion. Some hearing people may think this is rude, but in the Deaf culture, making and maintaining eye contact is a required and necessary practice.

Sign On

It is said that the eyes are the "windows to the soul." So think about what your soul wants to communicate!

Once you've engaged in conversation with a deaf person, maintain eye contact with her throughout the course of your dialogue. This is a way to experience direct communication. Because you use your eyes to "accept" and receive an incoming message, looking away suggests that you're not really participating in the conversation or do not wish to continue the dialogue.

Sign On

Eye contact can also be used as a turn-taking technique, especially in group discussions when everybody looks at the next speaker to begin a conversation.

If a hearing person breaks eye contact because of an auditory interruption (such as background noise or if someone else was to call to her), it is important for her to inform the deaf person as to why she looked away. The deaf person will think that something is wrong and will want to know what has happened to interrupt the conversation. If a hearing person breaks eye contact and looks at something behind the deaf person, the deaf person will turn to look also—thinking that something is going on behind her. If this happens, the hearing person should explain to the deaf person why eye contact was broken. Breaking eye contact without an explanation is considered rude in the Deaf culture, as the person will appear to be inattentive or not interested in the conversation.

What Do I Look at When I Talk to a Deaf Person?

While maintaining eye contact, you should broaden your visual perception to approximately 180 degrees wide. Meaning, concentrate on looking at her face and simultaneously take in signs that she is expressing with her hands. This is known as a "scanning" technique, in which you can receive all visual information at once through eye gaze. Over time, your eyes will become accustomed to focusing on one's face in front of you and still be able to receive signs presented to you from all sides around the face and body.

Sign Off

It is considered impolite to stare at someone's hands while she signs and to disregard her face.

It's Written All Over Your Face!

Of all the species, the human face is the most complex and versatile. You use your facial muscles as a means to visually display your attitudes, emotions, mood, opinions, and intentions. Facial expressions are powerful. The face can express your thoughts immediately—even faster than you can verbalize them. The muscles used for expression are mostly those in your forehead, eyebrows, eyes, nose, mouth, and cheeks.

Whether you're aware of it or not, you use your face to express feelings such as happiness, sadness, love, concern, embarrassment, surprise, fear, and excitement. When you say, "I am so happy that we won tickets to the game," chances are that your face will be lit up with a great smile. Even if you don't verbalize such an expression as "Oh, here we go again," the sarcasm will show itself on your face when you roll your eyes.

Here are some examples of how you use facial expressions:

◆ Smile (variations: half-smile, forced smile)
◆ Frown
◆ Squint
◆ Grimace
◆ Arch eyebrows
◆ Purse lips
◆ Wink
◆ Wrinkle forehead
◆ Smirk
◆ Twitch nose
◆ Bare teeth
◆ Bite lip
◆ Puff up cheeks with air
◆ Yawn

Clearly, appropriate use of facial expressions makes someone's behavior more predictable and understandable to others. Think about how difficult phone conversations can be when you're not face-to-face with the person and miss her expressions. The extent to which she is happy, bored, disinterested, or in agreement does not come across as clearly.

Sign Post _____

In 1972, research psychologists Paul Ekman and Carroll Izard traveled independently around the world to observe the faces of people and to see how different emotions were expressed. They found that some facial expressions were so innate and universal that even children who have been blind and deaf since birth display them: anger, disgust/contempt, fear, happiness, interest, sadness, and surprise.

In sign language, facial expressions are important. When watching deaf people sign to one another, some hearing people have expressed that they see the facial expressions as "exaggerated" or "excessively overstated." But that is because deaf people are indeed highly expressive when using their faces, which is the major part of the language.

Facial expressions play an important role in sign language. Not only do they express emotion, but they are also used to communicate things such as the introduction of a new topic (raised eyebrows), questioning (mouth open, squinted eyes, and eyebrows together), and emphasis (exerting more or less force when moving facial muscles).

 Sign On _____

Show that you are attentive by nodding slightly to your sign partner. If you are expressionless, it will convey inattentiveness.

It is imperative that feelings are shown on the face, along with the sign. For example, a signer would not just sign HAPPY with an expressionless poker face—This would actually mean that the person is not happy or is being sarcastic about being happy. A signer would sign HAPPY and simultaneously their face would lighten up and show a smile.

Another way that deaf people use facial expressions when signing is when they want to express the degree of something. If someone is very happy (elated), she would sign HAPPY and show a great, huge smile on her face. If she is just happy (glad), she would sign HAPPY with a moderate smile.

The following figures illustrate facial expressions and the differences between showing the expression of HAPPY, whether super elated or just glad.

HAPPY ("elated" facial expression)

HAPPY ("glad" facial expression)

I See What You Say!

In addition to focusing on your eyes, face, and body expressions, some deaf people will also look at your mouth to see what words or expressions you may be trying to form. They will follow your lip patterns (the shapes made by your mouth when you speak) to try and determine what words are being said. This is called speechreading. The old term for this was "lipreading," but this conveyed the idea that speech could be understood by focusing only on the movements of the lips. The term "speechreading" is more accurate because it recognizes that speech comprehension relies not only on the lips, but also the entire mouth and teeth in conjunction with facial expressions and body language.

Even hearing people speechread sometimes. Studies have found that if there is loud background noise, hearing people unconsciously will try to match other people's lip shapes to what sound they can hear. The next time you are in a very noisy room and can't hear the person in front of you, be aware of how closely you watch someone's mouth and visual cues to aid in understanding what he or she is saying.

Not all deaf people speechread. This is an acquired skill, and depends on one's education and exposure to this technique. When you use Contact Signing, you may notice that some people move their mouths to form English words along with signs, with or without the use of their voice. The choice of whether or not you do this should depend on the needs and preferences of your communication partner. Some deaf people who have speechreading and English skills will prefer that you mouth words, while others who do not have such skills may find it unnecessary.

> **Sign Post**
>
> In general, no more than 30 or 40 percent of the sounds of speech can be identified using vision alone. Try it yourself—turn off the sound on the TV (hit the mute button) and see how much you can comprehend through speechreading. See how difficult it can be?

Speechreading is not easy. Even the best speechreaders (those lucky few who can distinguish more than 30 percent of words) will miss words. English is known to be the most difficult language to speechread. Many sounds look alike on people's lips: B, M, and P look similar, as do F and V. It's also difficult to distinguish between CH, J, and SH. This means that words such as *bail*, *mail*, and *pail* look similar on the lips. So do *fan* and *van*, and *cheer*, *jeer*, and *sheer*.

> **Sign On**
>
> Look in a mirror and watch your lips as you mouth the words, *I love you*. Watch again as you mouth the words, *olive juice*. Looks the same, right? This is only one example of so many words and phrases that can look the same to a lipreader—It's tough!

Some sounds, such as K and G, are pronounced at the back of the throat. This makes words such as *key*, *kind*, *good*, and *girl* difficult to see.

Other factors can affect speechreading. Some people do not speak clearly—They may mumble or slur words. Others may have a heavy accent. Speechreading a man with a long moustache or anyone with an unfamiliar accent may also be difficult.

Here are some tips to help you as you're talking to someone who is speechreading:

- Make sure you have secured eye contact before you start speaking.
- Position yourself in good light so that your face is clearly visible. (Don't stand with your back to a light source or window; the light needs to be on your face.)
- Speak up if the person is hard-of-hearing, but do not shout; this distorts your voice.
- Do not exaggerate sounds when speaking; this distorts the message.

- Watch that your hands don't cover your face or lips.
- Don't eat food or chew gum.
- Thick moustaches and beards will also affect a deaf person's ability to read your lips.

Additionally, be aware of using too many unnecessary words when speaking. Speechreading calls for much energy and concentration. A speechreader may need to rest her eyes as she gets tired, or look away until she can regain focus.

Your Body Shows the Inner "You"

The way you stand and hold yourself says a lot, too. Are you uptight and stiff like a board or are you relaxed and loose? Do you appear to be unfriendly and distance yourself from someone, or try and appear more approachable and move closer to her?

One of the most important parts of nonverbal communication (meaning it's not spoken) is body language. It's a major form of nonverbal communication. Whether we're hearing or deaf, we use body language to pick up cues from another person's stance to give us more insight about her demeanor. And, more often than not, the other person is unaware of how much information she is giving off to us just from her body language.

> **Sign Post**
>
> Fifty percent of a person's character, ability to influence, and credibility is conveyed through nonverbal communication.

Think about it: If someone stands close to you, laughs a lot, and often touches your shoulder when speaking, you may perceive her as open, friendly, and fun. If someone glances at you coyly and positions her body a bit sideways, you may think that she is shy. Or if someone rests her chin on her palm and looks up at you from the top of her eyes and smirks, you may get the impression that she is critical and cynical toward you. Clearly, the level to which someone shows movement and expression gives you insight into her character—whether a person is conscious of this or not.

The following are some other ways that your body language reveals the inner you to others:

Action	Possible Interpretation of Personality
Firm handshake	Sure, confident, secure
Weak handshake	Nervous, shy, insecure
Tapping fingers	Anxious, restless, annoyed
Fidgeting (with hands or objects)	Bored
Retracted shoulders	Suppressed anger
Hunched shoulders	Feeling inferior, weak
Rapidly nods head	Impatient, eager to add to conversation
Slowly nods head	Shows interest and validation to speaker
Leaning forward	Interested, concerned, paying attention
Holding still	Heavy concentration in what you're saying
Mirroring your actions	In agreement with you
Clearing of throat	Nervousness

However, sometimes we can wrongly interpret someone's personality through her body language! For example, if someone moves around a lot and shifts her weight from side to side, you may view her as energetic and full of life. However, she may be feeling quite the opposite—uncomfortable and full of nervousness.

> **Sign Off** _____
>
> Another tricky body-language expression to interpret is when someone has her arms crossed. You may think that she is being defensive. But perhaps her arms are crossed because she is cold, or is trying to protect her body from physical harm.

Body Movements

When communicating with a deaf person, body movements are used as a part of ASL grammar, just like facial expressions. Body movements correspond to signs for specific grammatical information such as the degree of signs, feelings, and thoughts. Body movements are tied to signs for specific grammatical information.

The amount of body movements may seem exaggerated to hearing people (just as facial expressions may), but again, you will learn that it's all part of expressing yourself and getting your message across.

> **Sign On** _____
>
> The use of your face—eyes, mouth, facial expressions—must be coordinated with the use of body language and body movement when signing. The face and body are used to reinforce and support the meaning of your signs.

When signing, your body will serve many purposes, even in ways you may not have thought about before.

Showing Intensity

You can liken this to "volume" in hearing people's language. The amount of power and effort you put into your body movement (whether it's soft or strong, fast or slow) is comparable to the way you would adjust the volume in your voice (e.g., weak or loud).

To show intensity in a sign, such as if you were describing someone driving too fast, your eyes would squint as if you are driving furiously against the wind. Your mouth would be in a closed, tense form, and your body movement would show that you were stiff and tight. You'd sign DRIVE with your hands as if you are squeezing the wheel firmly and not wanting to lose control at such a high speed. To show less emphasis in a sign, such as if you were describing someone driving at a leisurely pace, your eyes would have a calm appearance. Your lips would be just puckered slightly and the body movement would show relaxed shoulders and body. You would sign DRIVE with your hands moving lightly and slowly as if you were at the wheel and driving in a relaxed state.

Here are examples of how your body movements would show a high or low intensity for the sign DRIVE:

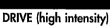
DRIVE (high intensity)   DRIVE (low intensity)

Showing Emphasis

You use body movement to stress the importance of a sign, just as you would use your tone in English to "make a point." Your body has the power to call attention to a sign or an action. To show emphasis, you would put more strength in your signing and movement. Head

nodding is also appropriate here, to convey the meaning of, "I'm right—I feel confident about what I'm saying." For example, if you feel strongly about expressing "yes," you would sign YES with full body and hand strength and a confident composure. If you're not really sure that you mean it, you would sign YES with a light, weak hand and body movement, and your expression would not be confident or certain.

Showing Negations

Hearing people and deaf people alike shake their heads side to side to mean "no," or if they are in disagreement with what a speaker is saying. In sign, shaking your head has an additional function. Simultaneously shaking your head "no" will give opposite meaning to a sign. For example, if you sign the phrase I CAN but add the head shaking, it will mean I CAN-NOT. This is another variation in sign so that you don't need to sign the word NOT; it is replaced by the negative head movement.

Sign Post

Showing negations in sign is a unique aspect of sign language. You can actually combine two different concepts into one sign to change its meaning. By shaking your head side to side, you will turn what you sign into a negative expression. So, if you sign WANT and shake your head NO, this means I DON'T WANT. Be aware of this when you shake your head NO in signing!

Asking Questions

Body movement is also used simultaneously with asking questions. If you were to ask a question that requires a "yes" or "no" answer, you would raise your eyebrows, slightly widen your eyes, tilt your body or head forward, and raise your shoulders.

If you were to ask a question starting with WHO, WHAT, WHERE, WHEN, WHY, or HOW, you would lower your eyebrows and pinch them together (almost as if you had a puzzled expression on your face), tilt your head, and bring your body and/or shoulders forward until you received a reply.

"Yes/No" Question Expression

"Wh" Question Expression

Where to Keep Your Hands When You're Not "Signing"

When you're not signing, you should keep your hands comfortably resting at your sides. Or, you may keep them in front of you with your palms interlocking. Be conscious that your hands "say" something; so, if you go to scratch yourself to relieve an itch, a deaf person's initial reaction may be to watch where your hands go for a possible message.

Sign Off

Don't keep your hands too close to your sides like a robot, or have them sloppily flopping around.

Signing Space

As you communicate with a deaf person, you'll be making and executing signs within your "signing space." This is the area in front of you, which is your personal space for arm movements.

Sign On

Your signing space can be likened to an imaginary box placed in front of your body, beginning from just on top of your head, down to your waist. Keep your signs within this box area. This is one time that you shouldn't be "thinking outside the box"!

Your signing space ranges from the top of your head area down to your hip area, and from your furthest reach to the right to your furthest reach left. Signs rarely ever occur behind you or much below your waist.

Sign Post

The signing space in front of the middle area of your chest is where you'll be doing much of your signing—It's where most two-handed signs are formed.

The signing space takes on great linguistic significance. You can indicate time, location, directional verbs, and pronouns and possessions, using your signing space.

Time (Past, Present, Future)

In sign language, a time sign will be used at the beginning of the sentence to indicate tense—past, present and future. Once a signed time tense is shown at the beginning of the signed story, there is no need to repeat the tense, as it has been already stated. If the story changes to a new time tense, then it needs to be presented and the story continues in that tense. It is one of the unique features of American Sign Language. In English, the rules are different! Verbs are changed according to tense.

To show that something occurred in the past, you would lean your body backward and use the part of the signing space slightly behind your body. To indicate that something is presently happening, stand straight and use the signing space just in front of you. For something that will occur in the future, you'll lean forward and use the signing space a bit further out in front of you than you normally would.

For the sign TO-GO, time tense will be established at the beginning—for example, YESTERDAY ME GO-TO STORE. The sign for YESTERDAY will indicate the tense for the rest of the sentence. There is no need to repeat the tense in the verb, as required in English. Another example to show future tense is TOMORROW ME GO-TO STORE. The word "will" is not added to the signs as the future tense is already indicated at the beginning of the sentence. In English, "will" is required to show future tense even if the word "tomorrow" is used at the beginning.

Also, in sign language, specific times are incorporated in the time tenses. For example, in the conversation, the sign for FOUR-MONTHS is signed in the future location of the signing space, which means "four months to come." To sign LAST YEAR, these two signs (PAST and YEAR) are incorporated in the past location of the space. Incorporated numbers with time tenses are also used to show number of days, months, and weeks. For example, TWO-WEEKS-AGO will be signed by using the numerical handshape for TWO on the palm forward motion ending over the shoulder for the sign, WEEK.

The following figures show the placement of your body to indicate time signs:

Past Tense   Present Tense   Future Tense

Location (Real or Imaginary)

We can use our signing space to describe whether an object is nearby or far from us. This can be used to show a real location or an imaginary one. For example, you can use your signing space to indicate whether or not a HOUSE is near or at a distance. To convey that a house is close by, you would put the sign HOUSE near your body. If the house is at a certain distance that's still easy to get to, place the sign in the middle area of your signing space. To express that the house is located far away, put the sign HOUSE at the end of your signing space away from your body. Another way to do this is to sign the word HOUSE first, and then point to an imaginary location in your signing space to indicate the relative distance of the house to you.

It is common practice to show imaginary placement of things by using our signing space. Signing at or just below our waist means that things are below us, such as the basement, submerged submarine, or an underground subway. If things are signed at our chest level, it implies that they are seen at eye level. Signs that are placed above our heads are for things that occur above us, such as an airplane or a bird flying.

Pronouns and Possessives

We'll also use our signing space to indicate pronouns and possessives. In sign language, the use of pronoun and possessives is unique. These signs can be used either in the presence or in the absence of persons, things, and places. Indication of pronouns and possessives is not random, but adheres to a certain location within the signing space.

Use your finger to point (the number ONE handshape) to a location within your signing space to show pronouns such as ME, YOU, HE, SHE, HIM, HER, IT, WE, US, THEY, and THEM. Where you point to show pronouns is not random. If the object is in front of you or around you, you can point to the object to indicate the pronoun. When the person is not present, you sign the gender of the person, and point to the designated location in the space. (See the following figure.)

Possessions make use of the signing space in the same way. They differ in that, instead of making the number ONE handshape, you'll use the SPREAD B handshape to show possessives such as MINE, YOUR, YOURS, HIS, HERS, ITS, OURS, THEIR, THEIRS. (See the following figure.)

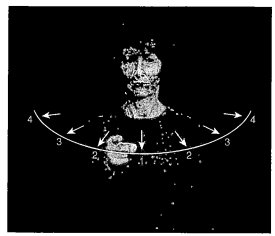

Pronoun Diagram
1 = YOU 2 = HE, SHE, HIM, HER 3 = IT 4 = THEY, THEM

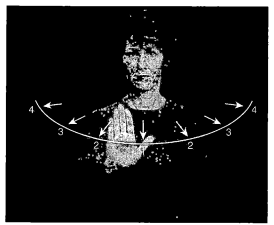

Possession Diagram
1 = YOUR 2 = HIS, HER, HERS
3 = ITS 4 = THEIR, THEIRS

Directional Verbs

In showing "who is doing what to whom," move your sign in your signing space to show the direction of the verb. You can directionalize many different verbs by moving your signs from one place within the pronoun location in the signing space to another.

The directional movement of the sign indicates the subject and the object of the verb. For example, if you sign I-GIVE-YOU, you would start the sign GIVE at your chest (to indicate

ME) and then move the sign in front of you toward the person (to indicate YOU). If they are giving something to you, you would start the sign GIVE at the outer side of the pronoun location (to indicate THEY) and end the sign at your chest (to indicate ME).

Other common verbs that are directionalized are LOOK-AT, HELP, GO, COME, FOLLOW, and BORROW.

> **Sign Off**
>
> Not all verbs can be directionalized. WANT is an example of this. If you were to sign SHE WANTS, you would point to the area just to the left or right in front of you to indicate pronoun (seen in the Pronoun Diagram above) and sign WANT as you normally would (at your chest area). As you communicate with other signers, you'll learn which verbs can and can't be directionalized. If in doubt, ask!

The Least You Need to Know

- ◆ Don't break eye contact with a deaf person until the conversation is over.
- ◆ While maintaining eye contact, use your span of vision to take in signs.
- ◆ Use your facial expressions and body movements to express grammatical information.
- ◆ Even the best speechreaders can't decipher every word, and will miss more than half of what is mouthed.
- ◆ Use both facial expressions and body movements to show intensity, emphasis, negations, and questions.
- ◆ Your signing space is the place where you'll execute your signs. You can use your space to show time, location, directional verbs, and pronouns and possessions.

In This Chapter

- ◆ Which hand to use, and when
- ◆ Your hands: Handshapes
- ◆ Palms
- ◆ Location
- ◆ Movement

 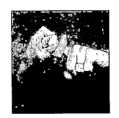   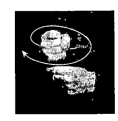

Chapter 6

Using Your Hands

You're almost ready to start signing! But, you still need to learn how to use your hands to sign effectively. Your hands are a powerful communication tool!

In this chapter, we cover what you need to know about using your hands. We review handshapes, orientation of palms, location of where a sign begins and ends, and hand movements. These are very important parts of a sign in addition to what you just learned about facial expressions and body movements. While this may seem overwhelming because it differs from what you experience using English, don't worry; this will make sense very shortly, and we believe you can *hand*le it!

Which Hand to Use?

Sometimes signs require the use of one hand, and sometimes both hands. When you make one-handed signs, you use your dominant hand. Your dominant hand is the hand that you use most often to write, throw, touch, and grab things. Your other hand is known as the constant hand. It's important for you to be aware of which is your dominant hand and which is your constant hand, as you will need to maintain this consistency when signing. If you're lucky enough to be ambidextrous, you'll have to pick which hand will be the dominant one and stick with it!

Use of One Hand

When fingerspelling the alphabet and signing numbers 1 to 100, you use one hand (the dominant hand). You also use your dominant hand to convey concepts such as pronouns (such as ME, YOU, IT, US, THEM) and possessives (MINE, YOURS, THEIRS, etc.). Additionally, you use one hand to sign GOOD, EAT, DRINK, HAPPY, WHY, SORRY (and lots more, too!).

Use of Both Hands

Sometimes both hands (the dominant hand and constant hand) are used. For many signs, the dominant hand does most of the work and is supported by the constant hand. For example, if you were to perform the signs STUDY, DOCTOR, SECRETARY, APPOINTMENT, and SCHEDULE, your constant hand would form a stationary platform for which the dominant hand will actively move on top.

There are also times when you use both your hands with equal effort, for example, to sign RAIN, SURPRISE, IMPORTANT, WANT, or SKIRT.

The Shape of Things to Come

In English, we use letters of the alphabet to form words. As a child, you memorized the 26 letters, which serve as a foundation for words that you either read or speak. In English, we combine consonant letters (such as D, T, R, S, P) and vowel letters (such as A, I, U) so that they become a word.

In sign language, we use handshapes (hand configurations) to form signs. The handshape is the most apparent component of a sign, just as letters are the most apparent component of an English word. Handshapes are determined by the openness of the hand, number of fingers extended, and manner in which the fingers are held. There are approximately 40 handshapes that serve as a foundation for creating signs.

The most frequently used handshapes are made with the same shapes used to form the manual alphabet and numbers (which will come right up in the next two chapters). However, linguists have identified a few additional handshapes outside of the manual alphabet and numbers that are also used to form signs. We've got the most common of these handshapes shown below so that you can use these as examples and be aware of handshapes when you start signing!

ON THE **DVD**

OPEN A

OPEN B (CLOSED 5)

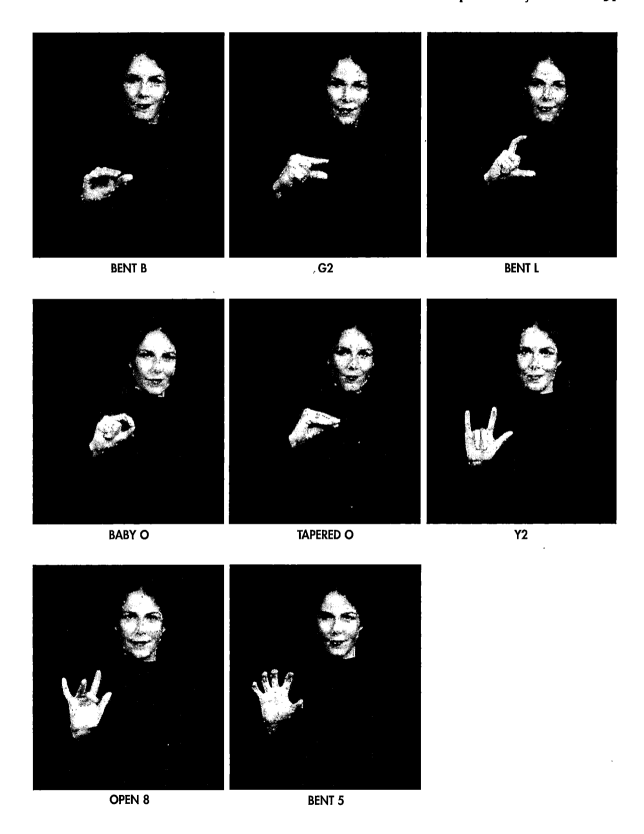

BENT B

, G2

BENT L

BABY O

TAPERED O

Y2

OPEN 8

BENT 5

Sign On

Using the preceding handshapes, the following are some examples of some signs in this book that use them:

◆ OPEN A. Used for GIRL, WHICH, TOMORROW, GAME

◆ OPEN B (CLOSED 5). Used for PLEASE, GOOD, YOUR, SCHOOL

◆ BENT L. Used for TIE, EYEGLASSES, PIZZA

◆ TAPERED O. Used for TEACH, HOME, FLOWERS

As you begin signing, you'll notice that sometimes handshapes will remain the same throughout the duration of a sign, and other times they will change from one handshape to another. You'll also note that sometimes you'll form one handshape with one hand, and a completely different handshape with the other. This is all part of the language of signs, and what gives each sign its distinctive meaning!

It's All Palms!

The direction that the palm faces changes the meaning of the sign. This is also known as the palm's "orientation." The palm's orientation is important because once the palm is faced in a certain position, the direction of the fingers and the back of the hand is obvious. Palms can face up, down, left, right, sideways, and in toward each other.

Examples of signs using palms face up are SERVICE, WANT, and BUY. Your palms are faced down for the signs HIGHWAY, TRAIN, and SIT. And palms face upright vertically toward each other for signs MEET, TRAF-FIC, and BALL. Palms can also face each other horizontally such as when signing PAPER, NICE, and SCHOOL.

Sign On

Review of the handshapes will help you to recognize the orientation of the palm, and assist in you in forming a correct sign.

Location, Location, Location

Location refers to where your arms and hands are placed in front of you within your signing space.

Some signs must remain in one location. For example, you use the upper part of your face (at the top of your head) for the male-orientated signs BOY, FATHER, and UNCLE, whereas GIRL, MOTHER, and AUNT are signed at the bottom of your face in the chin area.

Sign On

Some signs will stay in one location. For example, the sign for HAT stays in the upper head area. The sign itself would vary depending on the description of the hat (whether it's a cap, top-hat, visor, or bonnet), but it would remain at the head.

Other signs have a flexible location. If you were to sign COUSIN, you would form the let-ter C with your dominant hand and position it to show the appropriate gender—at the top of your head to indicate a male cousin or at the bottom of your chin for a female cousin. In between these two areas of your head implies COUSIN as a generic (non-gender-specific) term.

Another example is the use of the sign ACHE (which is also the same sign for PAIN). If you have a headache, you would sign ACHE at your head area; for a stomachache, sign ACHE by your tummy. ACHE can be signed for all locations on your body.

When you start signing, you'll notice that many signs that convey feelings are formed near the heart, such as LOVE, LIKE, FEEL, and TOUCH-HEART (SENTIMENTAL). You'll also see that signs showing cognitive concepts are formed near the head, such as THINK, KNOW, and UNDERSTAND.

Moving Right Along

There are basic categories of sign movements. Some are single movements and some are double. Single-movement signs will begin in one place and finish in another, within just one transfer. This means that your hands will start in a certain location and then "move" to a final location. The signs for WOMAN and MAN start at the head area and end at the chest.

Some single-movement signs are moved in a direction once, either on the body or in the signing space. On the body, signs include FEEL, HUNGRY, and THIRSTY. Single movement signs in the signing space include GO-TO, DRIVE-TO, and MEET-YOU.

> **Sign On** _____
>
> Some single-movement signs move from the signing space to the body or vice versa. Examples of signs that move from signing space to the body are KNOW, DRINK, and HAVE; examples of signs moving from the body to the signing space are LIKE, WATCH, and VOMIT.

If you wish to indicate a person driving along a winding road, you would sign DRIVE-TO as if you were actually driving through a twisting road. It would still be a single and direct movement but not in a straight path (as if you were driving on a highway). It would be in a gradually curved or sharp zigzag form (depending on the concept you wish to express).

Some double-movement (or twice-repeated movement) signs are used for signs such as MOTHER, UNCLE, and SCHOOL. Other repetitive movements would reflect the meaning of verbs such as EATING-ALL-DAY. The repetitive sign to show this concept of eating all day would be signing repeatedly in a circled form. In this book, you will see the sign for WAITING in a circled form to show the meaning that the person is waiting for a period of time.

Some signs have repetitive movements that may signal its plurality, such as by repeating a sign three or more times. As you repeat the sign several times, you may move from one location to another. For example, to sign TREES (FOREST), you would sign TREE several times (four or five) but move the sign slightly as you repeat each sign so that your communication partner can see that you are repeating the sign again and again to show multiple trees. This same concept can be used for signs such as BOOKS and HOUSES.

Besides the number of times a sign "moves," you will also note that some signs have visible patterns. Sign movement patterns include the following:

◆ **Circular Movements.** These movements are formed in "circles" in either a clockwise or counterclockwise pattern. For example, the movement of the sign PLEASE is in a circular form on the chest in a clockwise direction. For the regional sign SUNDAY, the movement of both palms facing outward in front of the chest space area is done in a counterclockwise circle. Examples of other circular movement signs in this book and DVD are SORRY, MUNDANE, and CLOUDS.

◆ **Back and Forth.** The back-and-forth movement is moving a sign from one location to the next location and then back to the original location along a straight line. For example, the sign BATHROOM moves back and forth twice in the chest space area. Other signs such as DOCTOR, TRAIN, and NAME will indicate the back and forth movement done twice. The difference of TRAIN and NAME is the palm orientation, but the movement is the same. The dominant hand will move back and forth on top of another constant hand.

◆ **Wiggles with fingers.** Put your fingers to work or "dance." Your fingers will wiggle for signs SNOW, COLOR, FIRE, and CANDLE. The wiggled movement of fingers reflects the meaning of moving objects. For the sign FIRE, your fingers wiggle to show the image of a flaring fire. For the sign SNOW, you can show a light snowfall by wiggling your fingers gently to indicate light falling of the snow. Or sign SNOW and wiggle your fingers fast and furiously to indicate a blizzard.

◆ **Curves.** Showing curves in movement is like forming an arc. For example, the sign DANCE swings from one location to the next location and back to the first location along a sweeping arc. It is similar to the back and forth movement but differs in that it is conducted in a visual semicircle form as opposed to across a visual horizontal line. Other examples are BLOCKS (STREETS), FINISH, and APPOINTMENT.

◆ **Waves.** Let us make waves with our hands! Think of a fish in water. How does a fish move? Some fish swim in a straight manner, such as a shark. Other fish move in a wavy, zig-zag fashion. The general sign FISH is a wavy movement across a visual horizontal line. Other examples of signs that use wave movements are WEATHER, FUNERAL, and ART.

In this book, we will show the movement of signs by using illustrated arrows and symbols on the photos. For those signs that are difficult, we have two pictures so you will clearly see where the sign begins and ends. Also, don't forget to use the DVD to see the movements clearly in action!

Is It a Noun or a Verb?

Sometimes the same sign is used for expressing either noun or verb versions of a concept. These are called "noun-verb" pairs. Not every sign is part of a noun-verb pair, but there are many out there. These signs will use the same handshape, palm orientation, and location, but will just differ the movement repetition to indicate whether it is a noun or a verb.

Sign Post

In noun-verb pairs, you use the same sign, but ...

◆ Verbs use a single movement and a bigger part of the sign space.

◆ Nouns use a double movement and a smaller part of the sign space.

Generally speaking, the verb in a noun-verb pair has a single movement and is signed larger than the noun. The noun in a noun-verb pair has a double repetition of movement and is signed smaller than the noun. When we sign the verb for FLY, we sign it once and big in the signing space. When we sign AIRPLANE—which is the same sign for FLY—we sign it twice with a smaller movement to show that it is a noun. Other examples are verb SIT (single movement) and noun CHAIR (double movement); verb EAT (single movement) and noun FOOD (double movement).

Putting It All Together

This chapter has covered the parts of a sign that you need to be aware of when using your hands. And, that's a handful of things to know! Now, let's see how this works when we put it all together and combine the face, body, and hand techniques we learned in this part of the book. Knowing these things will help you to get your signs across clearly and successfully. Over time, these things will be as natural to you as the back of your hand!

Sign ANGRY

◆ Face. Your face shows a frown on your forehead. Your eyes and eyebrows will be in a squinted position. Your facial muscles constrict to show the degree of anger. Your lips tighten up with teeth showing (if you are really angry).

◆ Body. Your body is upright and stiff with the feeling of being tensed with anger.

◆ Hand. Your handshapes are two BENT 5s placed on the chest area. The palms face toward the body. The single movement goes from the chest area up and outward in an arc-form.

Sign CLEAN

◆ Face. Your face will show the expression of feeling fresh and bright. Your eyes will open and be widened, along with the lips taking in a mouthful of air.

◆ Body. Your body will show the chest expanding to breathe in clean air.

◆ Hand. Your handshapes are two OPEN Bs placed in the signing space in front of you. Palms face each other horizontally, but in different positions—the constant hand is in an upward-facing position and the dominant hand is placed sideways on the constant hand's palm. The movement of the dominant hand is a single, sharp slide outward.

As you can now understand, sign language is a highly visual-spatial form of communication and also enables you to express yourself creatively!

And now, the moment you've been waiting for: You're ready to sign!

The Least You Need to Know

◆ The parts of a sign: handshapes, palms (orientation), location, movement—plus facial expressions and body movement, too!

◆ From fingerspelling to signing, your dominant hand does most of the work, and is sometimes supported by the constant hand.

◆ Most of the handshapes (hand configurations) used to form signs come from the American Manual Alphabet and Manual Numbers.

◆ Many signs will start in one location of the body or signing space and may "move" to end in another location.

In This Part

Part

Essential Basic Signs

Here we treat the basics in sign language (and the fundamentals in any language!): alphabet, numbers, and colors—with photographs (yes, these are photos of the authors!). By looking at real photos, you clearly see what your hands, body, and face express when you practice signs yourself. Also critical are the directives shown on each photo that indicate the direction of hand motion.

We've supplemented the photos with a DVD, located in the back sleeve of this book. Seeing Contact Signing in action is an excellent way to learn. The DVD presents signs and dialogues covered in Parts 3 through 6 of the book. Each sign will be shown in full motion—from fingerspelling to numbers to complete phrases and sentences used in conversation. If you are not able to understand the sign the first time, you can replay and watch it again and again until it becomes a part of you. A key to learning sign language is to practice, practice, practice!

In This Chapter

- ◆ The American Manual Alphabet
- ◆ When to fingerspell words
- ◆ Fingerspelling: A through Z
- ◆ How to position your hands and body

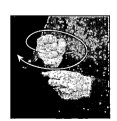

Sign Post _____

A form of fingerspelling has been used since the tenth century! Pictures found in Latin Bibles from the Middle Ages show evidence that monks used a type of fingerspelling among themselves. Given that they were forbidden to talk, they created a method of fingerspelling to communicate with one another.

Some signers use the alphabet to "initialize" signs. An initialized sign combines an existing sign with the manual alphabet handshape corresponding to the first letter of an English word. They may also be used to reflect a "made-up" sign between two people who have agreed upon this.

It is common for deaf signers to use initialized "sign names" instead of fingerspelling full names over and over. When meeting someone for the first time, you would fingerspell your name in its entirety. Then you would be given or asked to make up a sign name to use thereafter. For example, a person may fingerspell the letters C-Y-N-T-H-I-A to give her name, and then fingerspell the letter "C" and shake it in the air to initialize and create a sign name for CYNTHIA.

Sign Post _____

The first book that contained a manual alphabet for deaf people was published in 1620 by a Spanish priest, Juan Pablo de Bonet. Bonet believed that deaf people should learn a one-hand manual alphabet before they were taught to speak or speechread. His book was called *Simplification of Sounds and the Act of Teaching the Deaf to Speak.*

In each of the conversational signing chapters of this book, you'll see a section for words that may be fingerspelled. Many of these words can be fingerspelled for the purpose of emphasis, lexical signs (which are fingerspelled words "borrowed" from English), abbreviations, and if there is no sign for the particular English word. Look for these words and practice fingerspelling them!

Preparing to Fingerspell

Are you almost ready? You will use one hand to fingerspell the alphabet. Which hand should you use? The hand you use most frequently—your dominant hand. This is also the same hand you will use for one-handed signs (which we'll learn in the next part of the book!). Your other hand does not play a role in fingerspelling and can be kept relaxed at your side.

Sign Post _____

The American Manual Alphabet isn't the only fingerspelled alphabet in the world. Each sign language has its own alphabet. In America, one hand is used for fingerspelling. But some countries, such as Great Britain and Australia, use two hands to form letters in their sign language systems.

When you fingerspell (again, using your dominant hand), here's how you should position your body parts:

◆ Hold your arm in a relaxed and comfortable position at chest level.

◆ Bend at your elbow but keep your arm and hand straight up; don't bend your wrist.

◆ Ensure that your hands, wrist, and fingers are loose and free from tension.

◆ Keep your palm facing out, toward the person you're communicating with, and a little to the side so that a person can distinguish the letters being formed.

The American Manual Alphabet

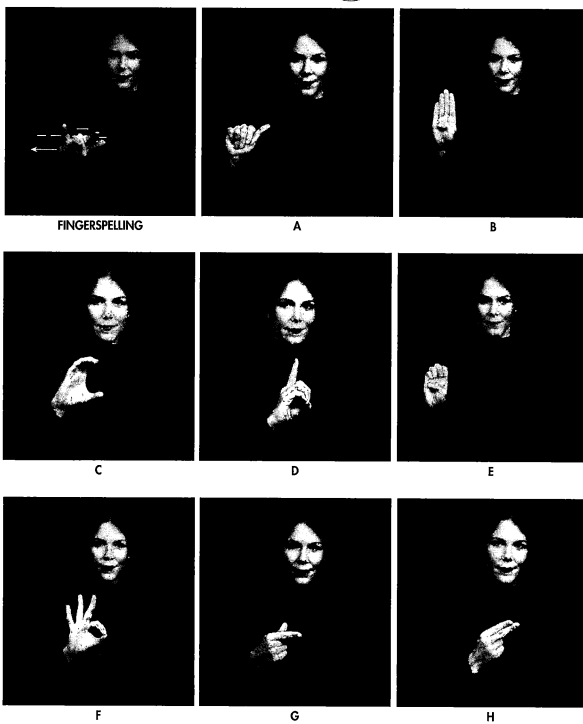

FINGERSPELLING

A

B

C

D

E

F

G

H

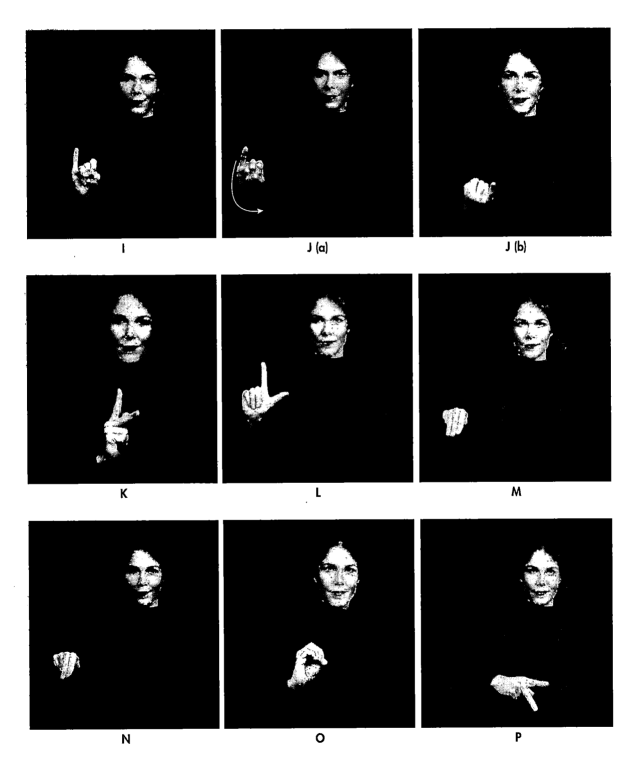

I

J (a)

J (b)

K

L

M

N

O

P

Q

R

S

T

U

V

W

X

Y

Z

Fingers in Motion

You're now on your way and you're doing great! It is essential for you to use finger-spelling at a normal pace. Too fast and the deaf person won't be able to catch what you're say-ing. Too slow and it would be like reading a word letter by letter. A very slow pace makes it difficult for your sign partner to put the word together.

To spell out a word, simply fingerspell let-ters one right after another and aim for a smooth flow. Make sure each letter is clear and distinct. If you are right-handed, you should fingerspell moving from left to right so that the person can read the letters you sign. This is done in a straight, horizontal line in your signing space. If you're left-handed, you should fingerspell moving from right to left. Keep your hand steady as you move across the sign-ing space.

Pause just a fraction of a second between words. This way the person knows that there is a break between words and it's not all just one long word.

Sign Off

When fingerspelling, don't do the following:

◆ "Mouth" letters. (But you can "mouth" the whole word while fingerspelling.)
◆ Bounce your hand or let it jerk around.
◆ "Watch" your hand as you formulate letters (you should be looking at the face of your conversation partner).
◆ Lift your elbow or make it stick out as to be distracting.

While fingerspelling the alphabet you'll notice the following:

◆ Some letters actually have a very strong likeness to the characters they represent: C, I, L, O, U, V, W, Y.
◆ Other letters may look somewhat similar to their print characters: A, D, E, K, M, N, P, Q, T.
◆ P is an upside-down K.
◆ J and Z are letters "drawn in the air."

When signing double letters, open your hand slightly for a brief transition. You don't have to put your hand down and then lift it up as to start over. To spell JJ, for example, just draw two Js in the air.

Sign Off

For beginners, the fingerspelled letters D and F often confused for one another. So are G with H, and E with S. Be aware of which is which.

The Least You Need to Know

♦ Use fingerspelling for names, titles, people, places, and brand names, and as a filler when you don't know a sign.

♦ Fingerspell at a normal pace—not too fast or too slow.

♦ Use your dominant hand for fingerspelling, whether it's your right or your left.

♦ Be relaxed and keep your arm at chest level, elbow slightly bent, and palm facing out.

In This Chapter

Chapter 8

Counting 1, 2, 3s

Now that you know your visual A-B-Cs, you need to learn your visual 1-2-3s! In this chapter, we'll show you how to sign numbers from 1 to 25, as well as some others that are frequently used. We'll also explain the ways to continue signing additional numbers on your own.

And for the first time, you'll be using both your hands to make some signs. Now, let's start counting.

When Should You Use Numbers?

We all use numbers everyday. When you're communicating with a deaf person, just as you would with a hearing person, you sign numbers for expressing the following:

◆ Address or street number
◆ Telephone number
◆ Age (even if we fib on it a little)
◆ Amount of money (dollars and cents)
◆ Credit card number
◆ Social Security number
◆ Score of a sports game or match
◆ Grade on a test
◆ Ingredient amount in a recipe

We just can't live without numbers, so you see why they're so important to learn!

Numbers

Signing the numbers isn't hard to learn. In fact, you'll see that many of the signs are sequential and use your fingers in a logical order.

Sign On _____

When signing numbers, keep your hand steady.

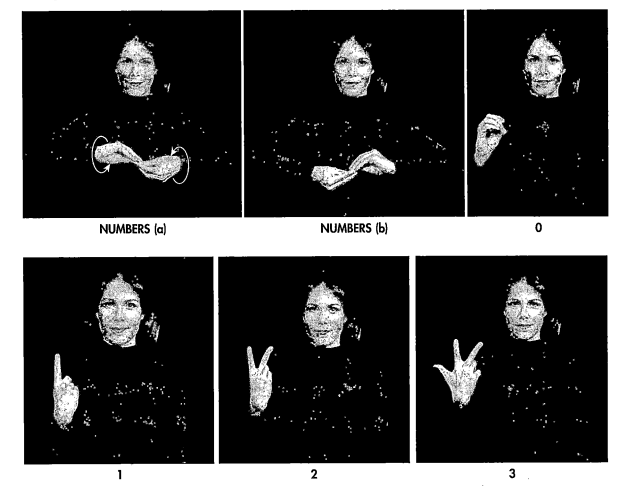

| NUMBERS (a) | NUMBERS (b) | 0 |

| 1 | 2 | 3 |

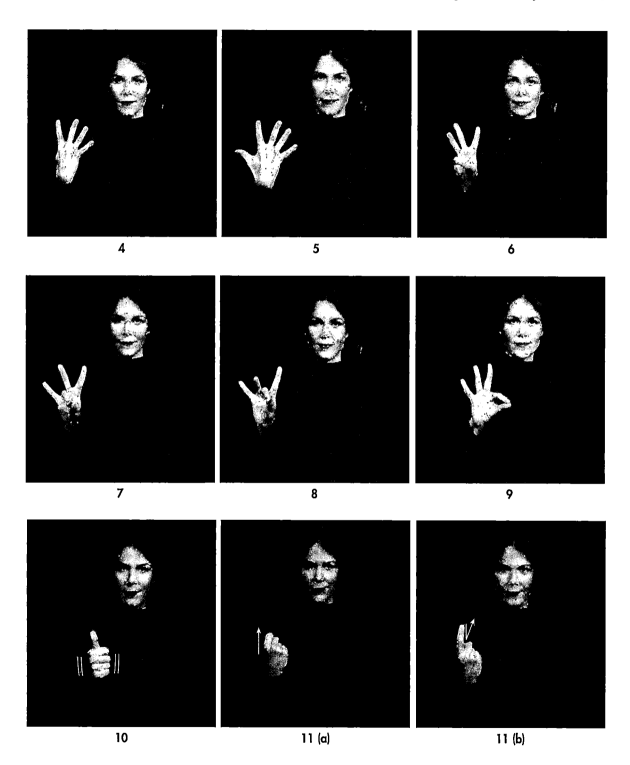

4

5

6

7

8

9

10

11 (a)

11 (b)

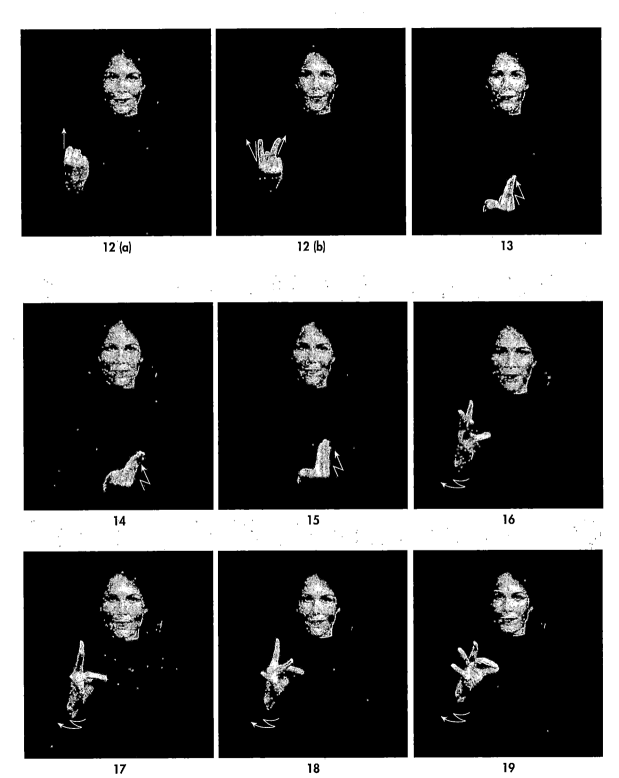

12 (a) 12 (b) 13

14 15 16

17 18 19

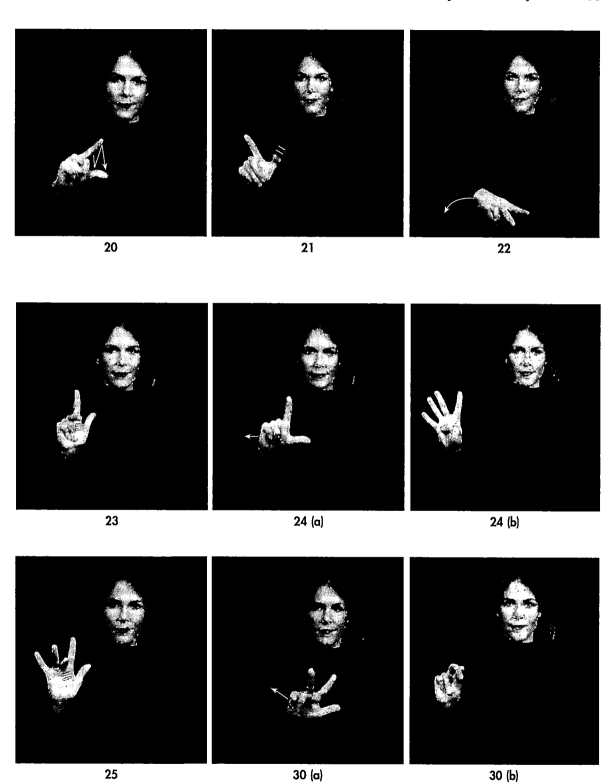

20

21

22

23

24 (a)

24 (b)

25

30 (a)

30 (b)

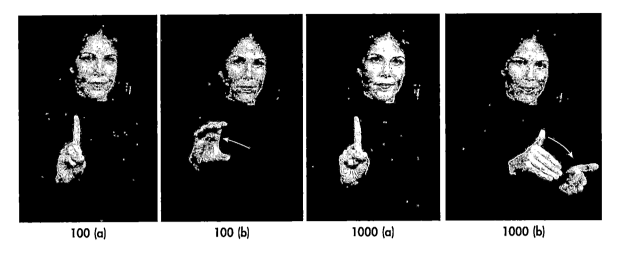

| 100 (a) | 100 (b) | 1000 (a) | 1000 (b) |

When signing numbers, you may recognize some similarities with some of the fingerspelled alphabet letters. The sign for the number TWO is the same as the sign for the letter V, but with a different palm orientation (for the number TWO , the palm faces in toward you). When signing the number SIX, you may notice that it closely resembles the letter W. You may also see that the number 0 is close to the letter O. What's the difference? When signing these numbers, you'll keep your fingers stretched and extended outward, with the tips of your fingers touching. The letters W and O are signed with your fingers slightly bent inward and rounded. For W, your thumb slightly overlaps your pinky finger. For O, your thumb slightly overlaps your first two fingers (index and middle).

Sign Off

Many hearing people in America who already use their hands for counting tend to make the letter W or number six instead of the right sign for number three. Resist the habit if this is something that you already do!

How to Keep on Counting

We've shown you the most common signs for counting, but, of course, the numbers are endless! You've learned how to sign 1 to 25 consecutively, but to sign higher numbers, here's what to do:

20. Use your index finger and thumb, and open and close them twice.

21. Think of the American "21 gun salute"— You sign 21 by using the L handshape and moving the top part of your thumb (just as if you were pulling the trigger on a gun!).

22 and double numbers (such as 33, 44, 55). Sign the number moving from left to right (if you're right-hand dominant) with the palm facing down. You sign from right to left if your dominant hand is your left.

23. Position your hand to number THREE, bend your middle forward in front of the hand, and move the middle finger up and down twice as if you are waving this finger.

24. This is created by two signs, beginning with the L handshape and then changing to the number FOUR handshape.

25. Use the FIVE handshape and bend the middle outward and move up and down twice.

26 to 29. Use the same pattern as the number 24. Use the L handshape first and then change to the next number.

Counting in the hundreds now! Numbers are borrowed from the Roman numerical system, using the C handshape to mean HUNDRED. For one hundred, we sign using the number ONE handshape with the palm facing outward instead of inward, as the next sign will follow with C. This pattern is the same for 200, 300, 400, 500, 600, 700, 800, and 900; you first form the number and then follow with the C handshape.

To sign odd numbers in the hundreds, you sign the first number and then sign HUNDRED (again, that's the handshape C), and end with the sign for the consecutive number(s). For example, for 307, you sign a total of three signs: THREE, HUNDRED, SEVEN. For 615, you sign: SIX, HUNDRED, FIFTEEN.

Sign Post

The sign for HUNDRED has its roots in Roman numerals! The Roman numeral C means 100.

A thousand involves two hands. Rules change here about the use of primary numbers. To sign 1,000, the number "one" handshape faces inward and then becomes a bent-B handshape, which ends at the palm of the constant hand. You sign numbers in a similar pattern as when you sign in the hundreds. For example, for 1,314, you sign the following: ONE, THOUSAND, THREE, HUNDRED, FOURTEEN (a total of five signs).

When signing more than just one number (for example, the year 2004), you start your hand a little left in front of you and slide it toward the right with each consecutive number signed. Orientation for these four signed numbers is outward. You can liken this to "number columns," as children learn when studying math—there is the ones column, the tens column, and the hundreds column. You create imaginary number columns in the signing space in front of you. Numbers, like letters, move from left to right if your right is your dominant hand and vice versa if you are left-handed.

Sign On

Breaking the rules! When using numbers to tell time, all numbers should be signed with the palm facing outward toward the other person (even numbers from one to five).

The Least You Need to Know

◆ You've already learned fingerspelling, so now you can sign your home address to a deaf person!

◆ Don't mix up signing the number ZERO for the letter O or the number SIX for the letter W. When signing numbers your fingers should be fully extended.

◆ Remember to break the rules and position your palm outward when using numbers to give the time.

◆ When signing multiple numbers consecutively, slide your hand slightly across your signing space.

In This Chapter

◆ When to sign colors

◆ Learning signs for colors

◆ How to sign shades of colors

    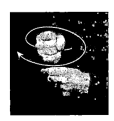

Chapter 9

Coloring Your Signs

The world is full of colors; some sights are vibrant, some are muted, and some fall somewhere in between. Colors give character and brilliance to all things around us. Colors can also have an emotional affect on us. Seeing yellow can make us feel happy and bright. Blue, such as the color of water or the sky, can be calming. As you read in Carole's personal story of *What it's Like to be Deaf*, the radiant beauty of the sun and trees outside with all of its colors "sings" to her with the same emotion you would experience listening to your favorite CD.

In this chapter, you learn signs for primary colors and practice using them, too.

When Should You Use Colors?

Signing colors is fun! Because deaf people are visually oriented, they often sign colors to depict the things they see. It is valuable to be descriptive as you sign, as it enriches the conversation.

You'll sign colors to describe people (such as eye color and hair color) and their attire (such as shirts, ties, jackets, and pants). Knowing color signs helps you to illustrate the environment around you—the sky, landscapes, houses and buildings, everything and anything.

Colors

When signing colors, we go back to using one hand—Yep, your dominant hand will be getting quite a workout!

Most color signs are initialized signs. Remember what this means? Many color signs use the first letter of the word and then make a sign out of it (through differing signing movement and location). You'll see that PINK and PURPLE use the handshape P for the sign, and BROWN and BLUE use the handshape B.

Now let's get to it and begin signing colors!

Sign Post

Some colors have interesting origins. You'll notice that the sign RED is in the lower face area, right below the mouth. This originated because our lips are red. The sign for the color ORANGE is actually the same sign for the fruit ORANGE, because of its distinctive color.

Now you'll be able to describe all the colors in a rainbow!

COLORS

BROWN

BLACK

RED

WHITE (a)

WHITE (b)

PINK

Chapter 7

Signing A, B, Cs

The alphabet is one of the first things you were taught as a child. The alphabet is critical to any language. In English, you use it to form words when writing and to spell out and clarify names and places of things when speaking with someone. Deaf people use the alphabet, too—called the American Manual Alphabet. It uses the same 26 letters as English, A through Z. Deaf people use certain handshapes to communicate each letter, known as fingerspelling.

As a hearing person beginning to study sign language, fingerspelling the alphabet is one of the first things you'll learn. It's essential to sign language—Even the most expert signers rely on fingerspelling to fill in vocabulary for which there are no signs. In this chapter we'll look at fingerspelling the alphabet and learn our visual A-B-Cs!

When Should You Use Fingerspelling?

Fingerspelling is used for naming titles, people, places (such as some states and cities), books, movies, and brand names of objects. It can also be used to "fill in" when you don't know a sign. When you're communicating with a deaf person and you aren't sure of a sign, use fingerspelling and she will show you the sign (if there is one—There may not be!). Note that some places across the country may have regional signs that you wouldn't be familiar with if you weren't from the area. Fingerspelling is also used for emphasis: If you want to call attention to a particular word, you simply spell it out!

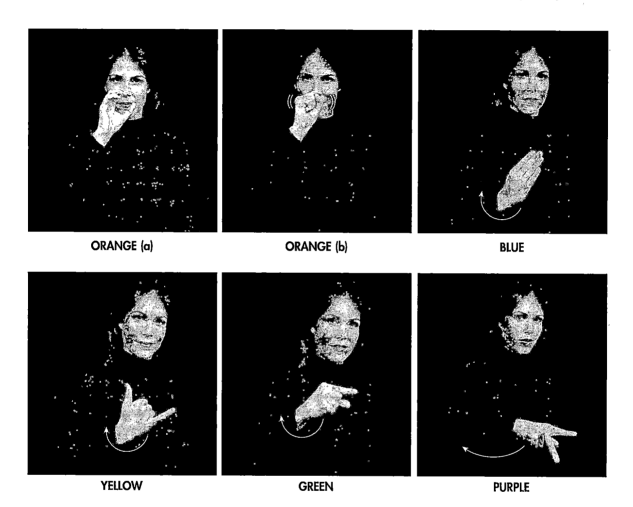

ORANGE (a)   ORANGE (b)   BLUE

YELLOW   GREEN   PURPLE

Are You a Shady Character?

There are many shades of colors. We can see a faint, light pink (such as baby pink), or a dark, rich pink (such a deep rose). How do you express shades of color? Here's where intensity of our facial expressions, body movements, and hands comes into play.

If you wanted to express LIGHT PINK, you could do so by having a tightened mouth and squinted eyes, and lightly touch your finger to your chin (to convey a feeling of softness). A shade of DARK PINK would be signed with a more powerful, intense body position, open eyes and more pursed lips. Your finger would more forcefully touch your chin as you show much more intensity.

Now that you've learned some of the basics of signing, the next chapters of the book will immerse you in conversational signs—These are things that you'll say to another signer. You can practice by yourself or we suggest practicing with another person. Either way, enjoy expressing yourself!

The Least You Need to Know

◆ As deaf people are highly visual, describing things accurately (including colors and textures) enhances a conversation.

◆ Initialization is used for most color signs.

◆ Use intensity in your face, body, and hands to show varying degrees, hues, and shades of colors.

In This Part

Part 4

Getting to Know You

In this part, you learn some signs to help you make "small talk" with deaf people. You'll be able to sign greetings, give an introduction and say a little about yourself, and sign goodbyes. Keep in mind that you can "mix and match" the sample conversation phrases and sentences—their uses are not limited to the chapters and can be employed in various settings!

In This Chapter

- ◆ Signing hellos and "nice to meet you"s
- ◆ Signing goodbyes
- ◆ What you should sign in a first introduction

Chapter 10

Meeting and Departing

In this chapter, we look at signs you can use when you get together with a deaf person and want to begin and end a conversation. You need to know opening and closing signs for conversations with your deaf friend, family, co-worker, and any other deaf person with whom you come in contact. This can take place in any setting, whether it's for social or business purposes. Some examples include parties, receptions or banquets, malls, banks, business meetings, in elevators, or school environments.

Now we'll look at some ways to communicate "hi"s and "bye"s. Let's get the conversations underway!

Greetings and Introductions

Conversations among deaf people are different from conversations among hearing people. Hearing people typically begin a dialogue formally and slowly as we try to figure out who the person is, carefully interviewing to assess her background, thoughts, values, and beliefs. The more that we know about the person up-front, the better able we are to figure out how to interact with her and avoid saying what could be culturally inappropriate.

Deaf conversational discourse follows a slightly different roadmap. Direct questions are asked rather than trying to ascertain values, beliefs, thoughts, and feelings.

To help you get started on the right foot, show your willingness to communicate. It will take courage to begin a dialogue and also to face the possibility of not being understood. It is not about the failure of your attempt to communicate. Your first step gives the dialogue an opportunity to break through the barriers. Find different ways of signing or gesturing to express what you wish to say, and deaf people will become your guide through this process, as they have been doing this all their lives. They are experts in their discourse navigation.

Sign On _____

Review Chapter 4 to remind yourself of the things that you should and shouldn't do when approaching and opening a conversation, engaging, and closing a conversation with a deaf person.

When you first meet a deaf person, you'll want to give a polite hello, your full name, and a courteous greeting. Identifying yourself as

hearing or deaf is important in the Deaf culture and expected in an introductory discourse.

Put effort into creating a balanced conversation. Ask questions and allow the other person to ask questions as well. Take turns when sharing stories and signing together so that one person does not dominate the conversation.

Key Conversational Signs

The following are some signs you can practice along with Carole and Dawn as they greet each other and introduce themselves.

English: Hello. What is your name?

CS: HELLO. WHAT YOUR NAME?

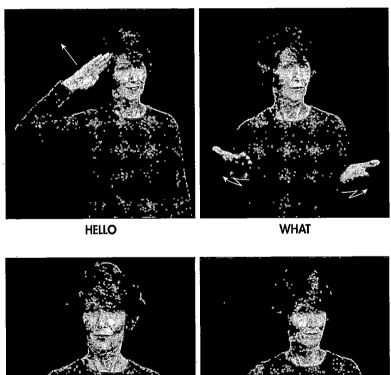

HELLO

WHAT

YOUR

NAME

English: Dawn. I am hearing and can sign.
CS: D-A-W-N. ME HEARING, CAN SIGN.

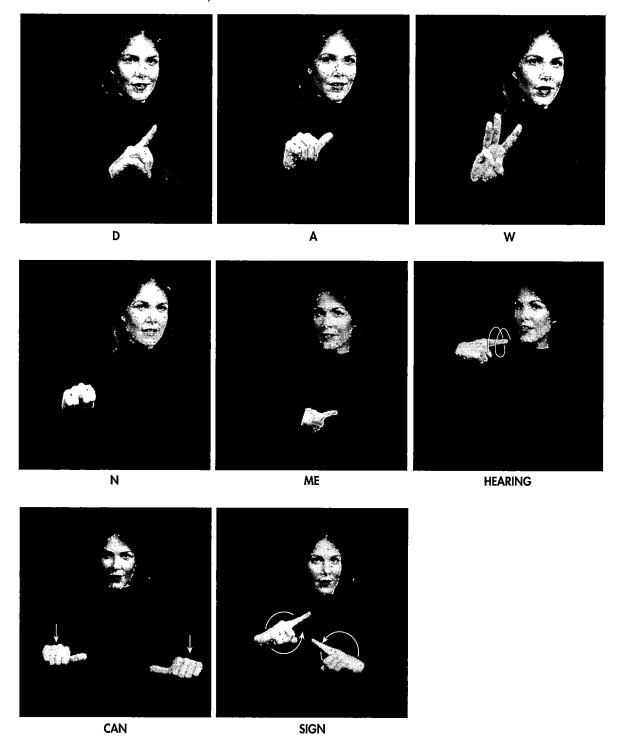

D	**A**	**W**
N	**ME**	**HEARING**
CAN	**SIGN**	

English: I'm Carole. I am deaf and speechread a little.
CS: C-A-R-O-L-E. ME DEAF, SPEECHREAD LITTLE.

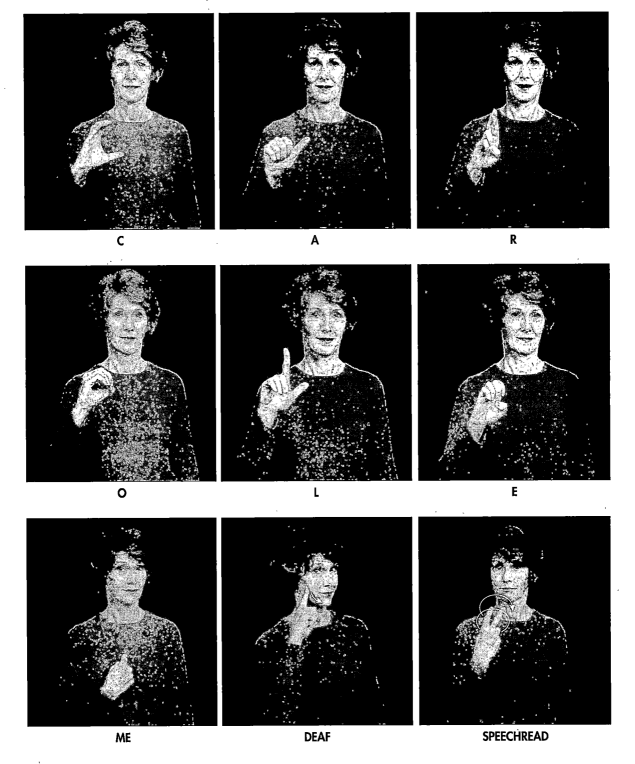

C   A   R

O   L   E

ME   DEAF   SPEECHREAD

LITTLE

English: It is nice to meet you.
CS: NICE MEET-YOU.

NICE

MEET-YOU

Sign On

For the sign SPEECHREADING, be sure to move your hands in a circle around your lips to imply *speechreading*. Be aware that moving your hands back and forth sideways is a variation of this sign that implies lipreading.

At a little airport in a small town, Carole and Andy discovered that there was no time schedule next to the six listed flights at a gate. Not being sure of how to proceed with this lack of information regarding the airline departure schedule, they approached an employee at the counter. They showed the person the tickets and asked how they would know when to board. The person stood paralyzed, not expecting to meet deaf people! It took a while for the person to regain her composure and write back to them, answering their question.

Sign Off

Do not freeze when you are face-to-face with a deaf person. Expect the unexpected and be ready to communicate!

Additional/Interchangeable Signs

MUCH (A LOT)

ON THE DVD

Fingerspelled Words

Fingerspell H-I for hi.

Carolyn Ball, President of the Conference of Interpreter Trainers (a national organization), gives advice for those meeting a deaf person for the first time with a sign-language interpreter present …

"Eye contact is very important in the Deaf world. When a hearing person meets or talks to a deaf person, it is important that the hearing person keeps eye contact with the deaf person.

"If a hearing person meets a deaf person and there is an interpreter present, it is important for the hearing person to maintain eye contact with the deaf person, not with the interpreter. Many hearing people do not know if they should look at the interpreter or the deaf person.

> **Sign On**
> Remember that eye contact is important: Look at the deaf person.

"When talking to the deaf person through an interpreter, you do not need say to the interpreter, "Tell her this." Speak directly to the deaf person as if you were talking to another hearing person. An example of this would be: "Hi Kelley, how are you today?" Do not say to the interpreter, "Please ask her (the deaf person) how she is doing."

"When the deaf person is signing her response to your question or comment, the interpreter will be speaking in English what the deaf person is signing. Remember to look at the deaf person when she is signing, not at the interpreter."

Goodbyes

Hearing people tend to end a conversation quickly and informally. We're busy, busy, busy, and in a hurry to go on to our next meeting or complete our next "to-do" for the day. If we need more information or follow-up with a person, we can simply dial the number on our work, home, or cell phone to contact someone anytime, anywhere.

When you say your goodbyes to deaf people, you will experience different departing behaviors from what you generally experience with hearing people. When hearing people say goodbyes, they tend to depart quickly without the need to look behind to check and see if the other person has also departed. Hearing people hear byes or other closing comments from behind them as they leave the site. To deaf people, this quick departure without looking back is considered to be rude. When deaf people say goodbyes, it lasts a bit longer. They may walk with the person to the departing point (e.g., to the car, to the door). It is not unusual to walk backward or sideways until both "visually agree" and confirm the final departure. If you are running late or need to depart quickly, it is appropriate to inform the person that you need to leave right away and also to add the reason(s) for such an abrupt departure.

> **Sign Post**
> In the Deaf culture, it is common for deaf people to greet and leave each other by giving a hug to the other person. As the Deaf community is close-knit, this action represents being in the Deaf "family." If a deaf person gives a hearing person a hug, it is a sign of welcoming into the community. Normally, when a deaf person meets with a hearing person the first few times, this does not take place and a handshake or a head nod is typically given.

Key Conversational Signs

The following are some signs that you can use to end a conversation with a deaf person.

Sign Off _____

There's no need to sign YOU and the end of the directional sign SEE-YOU; it would be repetitive, as the pronoun is already incorporated into the sign.

English: Hope to see you soon.

CS: HOPE SEE-YOU SOON.

| HOPE | SEE-YOU | SOON |

English: We look forward to seeing you again.

CS: WE LOOK-FORWARD SEE-YOU AGAIN.

| WE | LOOK-FORWARD | SEE-YOU | AGAIN |

English: Take care.
CS: TAKE-CARE.

TAKE CARE

 Sign On _____

TAKE CARE is the same sign for GOOD LUCK.

English: Goodbye.
CS: GOODBYE.

GOODBYE

Additional/Interchangeable Signs

ON THE
DVD

EXCUSE-ME

 Sign On _____

EXCUSE ME is the same sign for FORGIVE ME.

Fingerspelled Words

Fingerspell O-K for okay.

A Goodbye Story from Andy's Childhood

Andy shares with us a story about good-byes. When he was a little boy, often his hearing family and relatives met and socialized. Upon arrival, his aunts, uncles, and cousins would approach him to say *Hello* and *Good to see you*. Usually, the conversation would end here. Andy would go off to play or watch television alone while everyone chatted the day away. When the time came for people to leave, they would depart without saying *Goodbye* or *See you later*.

Sign Post

In Deaf culture, it is considered rude to leave the person without saying goodbye or at least informing the deaf person that you are parting.

Often, Andy would run out to learn that people have already left and he would be in tears and feel hurt. He felt that the relatives did not care about him or love him. He often wondered why people put an emphasis on greetings but not goodbyes. Ironically, at the Deaf school, goodbyes were different from the hearing home. Deaf children would take time saying goodbyes with hugs and smiles. These endings would feel more natural and warm to him as this put a nice closure to the visit or meeting.

The Least You Need to Know

◆ When first meeting a deaf person, be sure to say hello, state your name, and identify yourself as hearing.

◆ When conversing with a deaf person who has an interpreter, remember to look at the deaf person when you speak—not at the interpreter.

◆ Be sure to end a conversation with a face-to-face goodbye.

◆ Study the signs for greetings and farewells.

In This Chapter

- ◆ How to make "small talk"
- ◆ Building rapport
- ◆ A personal story about a first "Deaf encounter"
- ◆ Now you're talking!

    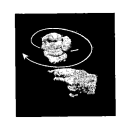

Chapter 11

Small Talk

So you've learned how to start and end a dialogue with a deaf person—Now you'll certainly want to fill in the middle part of the conversation and learn how to keep it going. After greetings and introductions to break the ice, you'll disclose a bit more about yourself.

In this chapter, you learn some cultural etiquette so that you won't feel tongue-tied (or should we say hand-tied?). You'll learn signs that will help you to feel comfortable and confident to make a connection with deaf people in any type of social situation.

Who Are You?

When meeting a deaf person for the first time, you'll want to share some background information about yourself. In Deaf culture, when a deaf person meets a hearing person, he needs to find out things such as who you are, where you work, where you grew up and where you live now, whether you know other deaf people, why you are interested in learning sign language, what you do in life and what your hobbies are, and learn about your marital status, your religion, and background.

The purpose of this direct questioning is to find common ground needed for communication and also for the possibility of developing a relationship. Deaf people will try to find the connection or relationship you may have with deaf people, interpreters, and the signer community. Some questions you may experience at the first meeting or the following meeting may sound too personal or direct to you. However, realize that this is the cultural means of gathering information.

Sign Post

A beautiful mind is one that willingly and freely seeks ways to blend others' differences into shared commonalities.

Embrace diversity! Dr. Gail Mellow, President of LaGuardia Community College, shares with us her thoughts on diversity …

"So many of us believe that being different is strange, or exotic, and all too often frightening. To create the kind of interconnected world that we want to live in requires that we move, either physically or intellectually, into unknown territory and encounter these differences. It requires that we embrace a new and more complex level of diversity, and that we acknowledge that moving outward toward new people and new experiences is an active and necessary part of our lives."

Key Conversational Signs

English: Where do you live?
CS: WHERE YOU LIVE?

WHERE

YOU

LIVE

English: My home is in New York City.
CS: MY HOME N-Y-C.

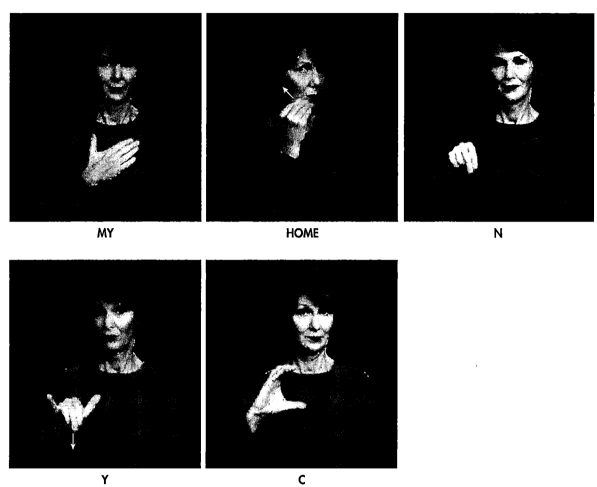

MY   HOME   N

Y   C

English: Where are you from?
CS: WHERE YOU FROM?

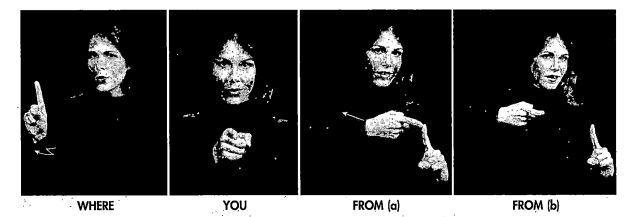

WHERE   YOU   FROM (a)   FROM (b)

English: I grew up in a house in New Jersey.
CS: GROW-UP HOUSE N-J.

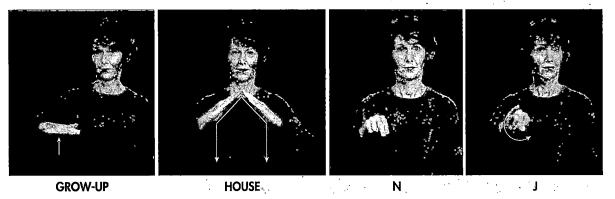

GROW-UP   HOUSE   N   J

Additional/Interchangeable Signs

FARM, REALLY (TRUE), DOESN'T-
MATTER, WHICH

ON THE
DVD

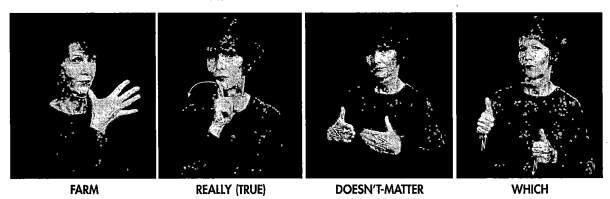

FARM   REALLY (TRUE)   DOESN'T-MATTER   WHICH

Sign On

Repeating the sign, REALLY with a questioning facial expression implies *are you really sure?*

Fingerspelled Words

Fingerspell A-P-T for apartment and C-I-T-Y for city.

A First-Time Experience Meeting a Deaf Person

Nicole Schroeer shares with us her experience meeting a deaf person for the first time and their mutual attempt to mediate the communication gap:

"I was working as a waitress in a New York City diner when I had my first "deaf encounter." A man was seated in my section. When I approached his table to take his order, the man animatedly gestured to his ears, shook his head, and looked expectantly at me. I was baffled. I mouthed "deaf?" The man gave me a smile and a big thumbs up. He then pointed to a fish item on the menu. He pointed to a picture of an orange, pointed to the fish, and mimed pouring, and then looked at me with a question on his face.

"I was confused but the man was clearly trying, and I felt I ought to as well. Having grown up in the 1970s, I had been exposed to deaf people mainly through Linda Bove on Sesame Street. I knew the manual alphabet and some bare bones signing. I fingerspelled S-A-U-C-E, and gave the man a "Is that what you mean?" kind of look. The man got very excited. He seemed really pleased that I could fingerspell and was trying my best to communicate with him. He pointed to the picture of the orange again. I pointed back to the orange and shook my head to indicate that there was no orange

sauce on the fish. The man smiled, and pointed to the fish on the menu with a definitive head nod. I wrote down his order and felt very pleased with my first "deaf interaction."

Sign Post

Put on a new set of eyes and communicate with a deaf person. Learn from each dialogue!

"When I brought the man's order to the table, he started signing to me, but I was lost. He gestured to my pad and pen. I gave it to him and he wrote, 'Me—Manny Williams. Live—3rd Avenue and 10th Street. 23 years old. You? Name? Live where? Old? How know sign?' He seemed eager to chat. Instantly my well-intentioned will to communicate left me as my "weirdo detector" went off. Who was this guy to give me his last name and address, and to want to know mine?! In New York City you practically have to be engaged before sharing your address with someone. Was this guy trying to pick me up? Was he a stalker? I tersely wrote back, "Sign from Sesame Street," and rushed off to tend to the rest of my tables. The man tried to get my attention again, but I studiously avoided his gaze. When he was finished with dinner he asked me what shifts I worked. I avoided giving him an exact answer, now confirmed in my belief that he was some sort of sleazy, unstable stalker.

"It was only years later when I began taking courses in American Sign Language and socializing in the Deaf community that I understood the impact of that transaction. The full, formal introduction of first and last name, as well as the address and age were simply identifying information and considered polite in the Deaf community. Now the idea of giving only my first name to a deaf person seems downright rude. I also now understand the excitement of finding a service professional who was open to signing. Wanting to know my shift hours had less to do with the deaf man's excitement over me personally than with his excitement at the idea of being able to go into a restaurant, have questions answered, have a chat, and be served by someone who can communicate with him. Had I been aware of the impact of this information at the time, my interaction with this man may have transpired very differently. Manny Williams could have had a comfortable, friendly neighborhood diner to frequent, and I would have had a loyal customer."

Key Conversational Signs

English: How are you?

CS: HOW YOU?

What's New?

When socializing with a deaf person, you'll want to ask him how he's doing and also chat about what you've been up to. You're building a relationship with the person.

To begin a relationship, find common ground, hobbies, topics of interest, and fun things you both like to do. Once you find a topic that you can converse about, you will be able to build on the relationship.

HOW   YOU

English: Fine. What's up?

CS: FINE. WHAT'S-UP?

Sign On

Some parts of America sign FINE once; and other parts sign the hand movement twice.

FINE   WHAT'S-UP

English: Everything's the same; nothing's new.
CS: EVERYTHING SAME (MUNDANE) NOTHING NEW.

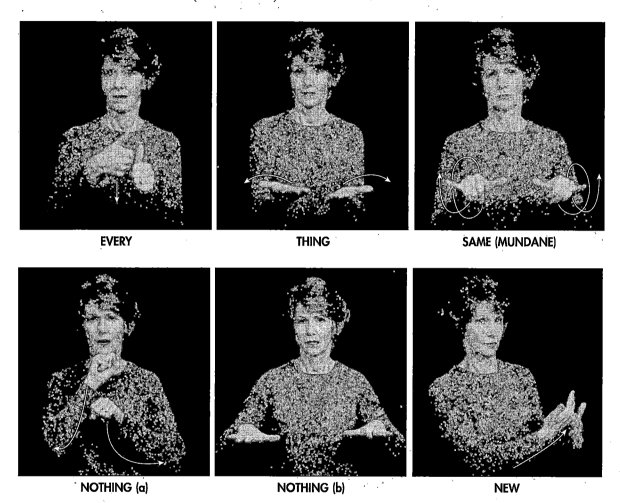

EVERY · THING · SAME (MUNDANE)

NOTHING (a) · NOTHING (b) · NEW

Additional/Interchangeable Signs

OLD, KNOW, WHAT-DO, PLEASE, TELL-ME, INFORM-YOU

OLD (a)	OLD (b)	KNOW
WHAT-DO	PLEASE	TELL-ME

Sign Off

Use the pronoun space as illustrated in Chapter 5. The directional verb sign TELL-ME moves in the direction from *you* to *me*. Another example is INFORM-YOU; the movement of this sign starts from *me* and ends at *you* in the pronoun space.

However, do not confuse signers by signing the three separate signs for YOU, TELL, ME. This will appear in English as *you, tell you, me.*

INFORM-YOU (a)

INFORM-YOU (b)

Fingerspelled Words

Fingerspell N-W-S for news, Y-S for yes (when emphasized), and N-O for no (when emphasized).

The Least You Need to Know

◆ Deaf people may seem direct in their questioning to get to know you; that is their cultural way of gathering information.

◆ Be aware of local or regional variations for signs

◆ Make every encounter with a deaf person a positive and learning experience for both of you.

◆ Be open to communicating; use a combination of signs and gestures.

In This Chapter

- ◆ Time on your hands
- ◆ Signs for time, calendar, weather
- ◆ Deaf culture and the value of time
- ◆ Weather the storm

More Small Talk

Every day we talk about things pertaining to time of day, calendars, and weather. These things keep us on track with our current schedules, plans, and events that will occur weeks ahead. We talk about the time and calendar when scheduling our daily activities: when to catch a bus or train, arrive at a destination, or meet with another person. Weather is another instrumental factor influencing our lives. We need to know the forecast so that we can dress accordingly (bringing an umbrella if needed). Also, we need to know if unexpected weather conditions such as bad storms, hurricanes, and tornadoes are probable, so that we can make alternative plans.

Certainly, time, calendar, and weather are topics of conversation that we have with others on a daily basis—and sometimes several times a day! So now you'll learn more "small-talk" signs.

Time

Time is important to all people. However, cultures place varying emphasis on timeliness. In the American hearing culture, because it is such an individualistic society, there is a heavy emphasis on timeliness. Arriving late or overstaying your welcome is considered rude.

In the American Deaf culture, though, because deaf people value spending time with others with whom they can easily communicate and develop friendships with, you can expect long hellos and goodbyes sandwiching in hours of catching up.

Key Conversational Signs

English: What time is it?
CS: WHAT-TIME?

WHAT-TIME

 Sign On _____

Some parts of America sign WHAT-TIME as one sign while other may use two signs: WHAT, TIME.

 Sign On _____

In expressing time, rules change for the use of the manual number signs. The orientation of the palm for signing time numbers from ONE to NINE will face outward.

 Sign On _____

Deaf people talk about time a little differently than people who can hear. In English, it is common to say something like: "half past 11:00," "quarter till 10:00," or "10 till 9:00." In sign language, time needs to be given as it is exactly on the clock. Using these examples, you would sign "11:30," "9:45," and "8:50," respectively. Remember also to sign time by tapping an imaginary watch on your wrist first and then sign the time. (Lynne Eighinger, Signs of Development).

English: It's 7:03 in the morning.
CS: 7:03 MORNING.

7	0	3	MORNING

English: I am late!
CS: ME LATE!

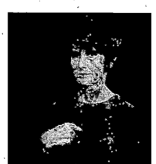

ME   LATE

Additional/Interchangeable Signs

AFTERNOON, NIGHT, SLEEP, AWAKE, MORE, TIRED

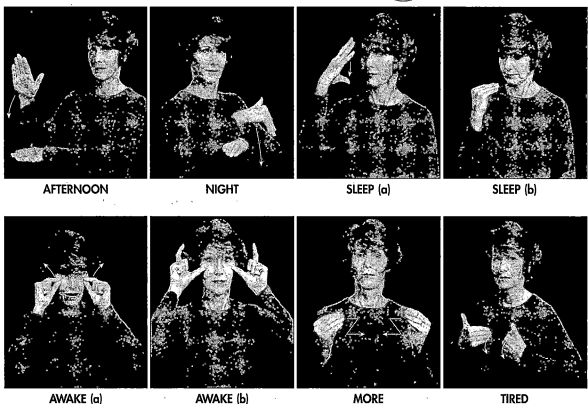

| AFTERNOON | NIGHT | SLEEP (a) | SLEEP (b) |
| AWAKE (a) | AWAKE (b) | MORE | TIRED |

Fingerspelled Words

Fingerspell L-A-T-E for late and E-A-R-L-Y for early.

Deaf Culture's Value of Time

The following story comes to us from Katherine Dudina, a New York City sign-language interpreter, as she reflects upon her experience with the concept of time in the Deaf culture ...

"As a new signer I had always craved more interaction with the members of the Deaf community. There is no better way to learn a new language than by placing yourself in the environment where that language is used. I attended holiday parties, lectures, classes, and any other events involving ASL.

"One such event was a monthly gathering at a Russian club for the Deaf. The flyer advertised the time as '6:00 P.M. till ???' So I showed up at 6:00 on the dot—I didn't want to be late and miss all the fun. "When I arrived at the club, I thought I had made a mistake; there was no one there but me, alone in a large well-lit room with a few tables and chairs. I checked the flyer again to confirm the location. No, this was correct. Had the event been cancelled? Just as I was thinking this, a man arrived. He looked at me suspiciously and signed, 'Deaf?'

"'No,' I responded, 'I came to the Russian club for the Deaf.'

"'Oh,' he laughed, 'Then have a seat—Enjoy.'

Sign Post

Because many deaf people are community-oriented, gathering as often as possible is valued more than gathering on time. Time is more fluid and not adhered to as rigidly as in the rest of the American society. A common attitude is "Let it be natural and things will happen when they happen."

"I took a seat, as I was told, and remained there for the next four hours. It wasn't until then that the rest of the participants started to arrive. At around midnight the party reached its pinnacle. There were families with children as young as three years old, senior citizens, and all ages in between. People divided into little groups where friendly rumors, games, and heated—but silent— discussions were being shared. During my first visit I could not participate—The culture shock was too great. It was fascinating just to watch. The only accurate part of the flyer was the end time. The event definitely lasted until '???' At 1 A.M., I was one of the first people to leave, thinking about my unusual cultural experience all the way home."

Calendar

Our life activities and events go by the calendar! Dates are essential for many of us who have the tendency to plan ahead. Important events such as parties, gatherings, appointments, and meeting dates need to be recorded in our calendars. There are lots of ways we keep track of our scheduling, too—whether the method we use is paper-based (in a calendar book), electronic-based (such as with a hand-held Personal Digital Assistant (PDA), or a software program used in our personal computers).

For some deaf people who do not have access to phones, computers, or pagers, face-to-face appointments need to be made. The following conversation typically takes place in offices and work places.

Key Conversational Signs

English: I need to make an appointment.
CS: NEED APPOINTMENT.

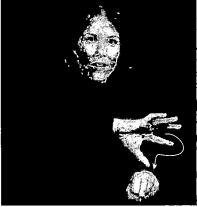

NEED   APPOINTMENT (a)   APPOINTMENT (b)

English: Just a moment ... Checking the schedule.
CS: JUST-A-MOMENT ... CHECK SCHEDULE.

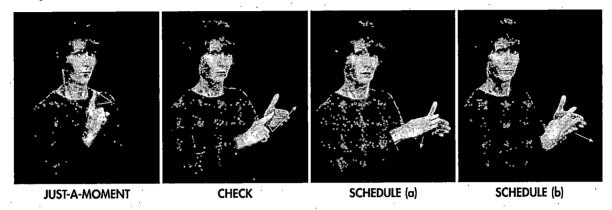

| JUST-A-MOMENT | CHECK | SCHEDULE (a) | SCHEDULE (b) |

English: Is tomorrow night good?
CS: TOMMORROW NIGHT GOOD?

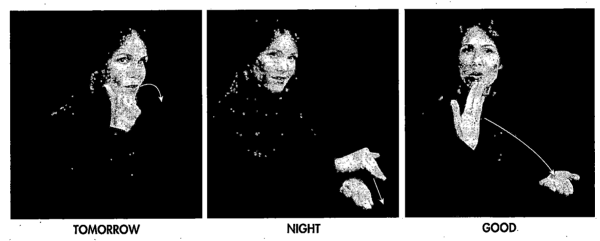

| TOMORROW | NIGHT | GOOD |

English: Wednesday is better.
CS: WEDNESDAY BETTER.

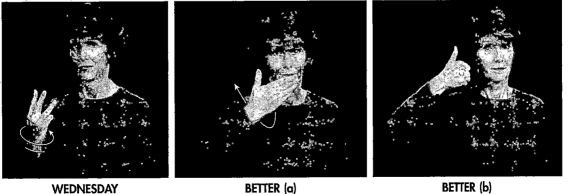

| WEDNESDAY | BETTER (a) | BETTER (b) |

Additional/Interchangeable Signs

WEEK, DAY, MONDAY, TUESDAY, FRIDAY, SATURDAY, SUNDAY, MONTH, YEAR, YESTERDAY, TODAY, CANCEL

| WEEK | DAY | MONDAY | TUESDAY |

| FRIDAY | SATURDAY | SUNDAY | MONTH |

| YEAR | YESTERDAY | TODAY | CANCEL |

Sign On

When signing about days of the week, the fingers of the nondominant (usually the left) hand become the weeks of the calendar. This visual set-up makes it very clear during which week of the month something will occur. ASL works very efficiently in this way. Dates can also be given by signing an abbreviation for the month, such as J-A-N for January, F-E-B for February, and so on, and then signing the number for the day of the month. (Lynne Eighinger, Signs of Development)

Sign On

Signs for SUNDAY and MONDAY vary from region to region in America. Ask a deaf person which signs are used in your area.

Sign On

The difference between TODAY and NOW is the movement; TODAY is a double movement, and NOW is a single movement.

Fingerspelled Words

Fingerspell T-H for Thursday, D-A-T-E for date, J-A-N for January, F-E-B for February, M-A-R-C-H for March, A-P-R-I-L for April, M-A-Y for May, J-U-N-E for June, J-U-L-Y for July, A-U-G for August, S-E-P-T for September, O-C-T for October, N-O-V for November, and D-E-C for December.

In Deaf culture, life revolves around activities in one's calendar. There are Deaf activities such as bowling, women's club, holiday parties, etc. For general deaf activities, such as interpreted theatrical shows, cultural events, conferences, and parties, the calendar plays an important role in making such plans. Deaf Clubs across America (local and national organizations) distribute calendars that list Deaf/deaf events and activities sponsored by the Clubs. These events are special and not to be forgotten or missed!

Weather

The Deaf culture is regarded as a "high-context" culture. High-context cultures are group oriented, and form tight, close, personal relationships. There is extensive information sharing within the Deaf community and with friends and families. Value is placed on people and taking someone's word as the truth. The nature of information shared is very detailed, deeper than what is shared in a hearing conversation.

When deaf people with established relationships come together, they often share details in narrative form. When a hearing person meets a deaf person, there are cultural differences in conversational highlights. This means that what is considered important to a hearing person (e.g., "I arrived late to work because I overslept") might be explained by her deaf colleague with details of the event before, such as "worked too late, arrived home to a sick baby, faced a grouchy spouse, missed the bus, dropped her briefcase," and so forth.

Sign Post

The Deaf, Japanese, Mediterranean, Arab, and Latin cultures are high-context. Low-context cultures include North American, Canadian, German, Swiss, Scandinavian, and other Northern Europeans.

Additionally, deaf people take it upon themselves to share information regarding the hearing majority culture with other deaf people. Sometimes hearing people may watch deaf people signing to each other while a speaker is talking, and interpret this as being rude—likening it to seeing two people whispering during a speaker's presentation and not paying attention. But the reality is that deaf people do this to help each other understand information. It is the usual practice that a deaf person who understands a hearing person's message is obligated to pass along that message to those deaf people who do not understand.

The American hearing low-context culture places more emphasis on the individual, where personal relations are more fragmented and compartmentalized from each other.

All of this reiterates the importance for you to be a giver of information and to share knowledge and experiences in conversations with deaf people.

Key Conversational Signs

English: What's the weather?
CS: WHAT WEATHER?

 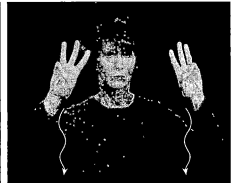

WHAT   WEATHER

English: It's rainy, cold, and windy.
CS: RAINY, COLD, WINDY.

RAINY   COLD   WINDY

English: I wish it was sunny and warm.
CS: WISH SUNNY, WARM.

WISH

SUNNY

WARM

Additional/Interchangeable Signs

TEMPERATURE, CLOUDS, SNOW, COOL,
WET, HOT, DRY, SUN, MOON, STARS

ON THE
DVD

TEMPERATURE

CLOUDS

SNOW

Sign Post

The sign CLOUDS may be signed differently depending on the shape and
type of clouds seen.

COOL   WET (a)   WET (b)

HOT   DRY (a)   DRY (b)

SUN   MOON   STARS

Sign On

A variation for SUN may include first fingerspelling S-U-N and then using the sign SUN.

Fingerspelled Words

Fingerspell I-C-E for ice, S-U-N for sun, and H-O-T for hot (when emphasized).

New Technology for Weather Alerts

In Oklahoma, deaf and hard-of-hearing people can now receive hazardous weather information directly from the National Weather Service (NWS). The program, called OK-WARN (Oklahoma Weather Alert Remote Notification), supports a system that serves the Deaf community statewide. OK-WARN is a customized database that sends out critical weather information to alphanumeric pagers and e-mail addresses. When the NWS issues a weather alert, the program will automatically send a message to all participating pagers, so notification is instant. They receive forecasts, watches, and warnings as well as information about tornadoes, thunderstorms, winter storms, flash floods, river floods, and high winds. OK-WARN is believed to be the only program in the United States that directly relays NWS alerts through pagers to people who are deaf or hard-of-hearing.

Editor Matthew Broaddus of the Sapulpa Daily Herald (Sapulpa, Oklahoma) wrote that the original idea for OK-WARN came from Vincent "Bim" Wood, a deaf man who conducted a nine-month survey following a tornado outbreak. His survey found that 81 percent of deaf and hard-of hearing people have experienced fear about being unprepared for weather emergencies.

Sign Post

There are devices that alert deaf people about weather warnings. The NOAA Weather Radio (NWR) has a receiver system that can be connected to the existing security system or the alerting system, such as a doorbell, smoke detector, or other sensors. Some NRW receivers can be programmed to set off an alarm for events such as tornadoes, flash floods, hurricanes, and local civil emergencies. In some states, there are local plans for such emergency evacuations for deaf people.

Wood spoke with many Oklahomans who had been caught off-guard by hazardous weather, including a deaf man who fortunately took shelter after speechreading only the word "closet" during a televised weather alert. The program has been successful and well received. Hopefully, other states will follow suit and alert their Deaf communities of weather disasters.

The Least You Need to Know

- Time and schedules are not adhered to as closely in the Deaf community as in the hearing community.
- The Deaf culture is regarded as a "high-context" culture.
- Deaf people may often rely on face-to-face meetings for scheduling an event if they are not able to communicate via phone, pager, or Internet.
- Special pagers enable deaf people to receive hazardous-weather information directly from the National Weather Service (NWS).

In This Chapter

- ◆ Signs for the immediate and extended family
- ◆ "90 percent" facts of deaf family life
- ◆ Deafness in American families
- ◆ Life stories from two CODAs and parents of CODAs

Family

Few things can compare with the importance of family. Your family is a part of you and will be there throughout your life. You are who you are today because of the way your family has raised you and shaped your thinking from an early age.

Family members want the best for you, and try to instill values in you by teaching what is right and what is wrong during your childhood. There's a lot of love and time that went into your development. Even as adults, we remember theories or sayings from our grandparents, parents, siblings, or cousins. Their words can leave an impact upon us for a lifetime!

In this chapter, you'll learn signs to identify those in your family circle. You may introduce your family members in a variety of places, including family gatherings and outings, dinners, parties, activities, and events.

It's All in the Family!

Survey results show some interesting information that is referred to as the "Ninety Percent Facts of Deaf Family Life." Although 90 percent is an approximation (actual study results range from 87 to 96 percent for each of the facts), this gives you a good understanding of the presence of deafness in American family life. Approximately 90 percent of deaf children grow up in hearing families; 90 percent of deaf people marry other deaf people; and 90 percent of children born to deaf couples are hearing.

Given this, there will sometimes be a "rub" resulting from cultural clashes. Deaf children may feel isolated or rejected by hearing family members. Deaf people may marry other deaf people and exclude other family members from their safe, familiar nuclear unity. Hearing children of deaf parents may be confused about their dual identity and confused about their loyalty to the Deaf community or the hearing community. However, this family picture is changing slowly as more hearing members are learning how to sign! As you meet people who are deaf (or whose parents are deaf), be sensitive to their different family life experiences.

Here are some conversational signs that you can use when you're communicating with a deaf person and want to introduce your family.

Key Conversational Signs

English: I am introducing my husband.
CS: INTRODUCE MY HUSBAND.

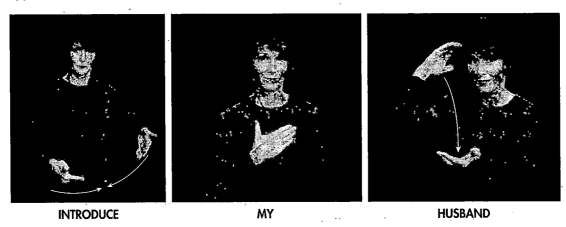

INTRODUCE   MY   HUSBAND

English: I'm happy you are here. This is my mother and father.
CS: HAPPY (GLAD) YOU HERE. THIS MOTHER, FATHER.

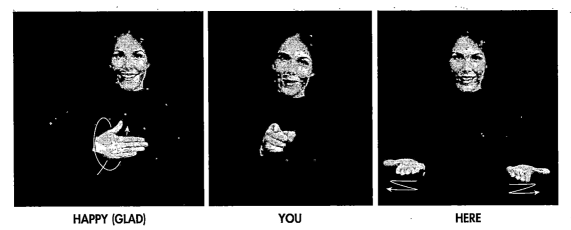

HAPPY (GLAD)   YOU   HERE

THIS   MOTHER   FATHER

English: Do you have children?
CS: YOU HAVE CHILDREN?

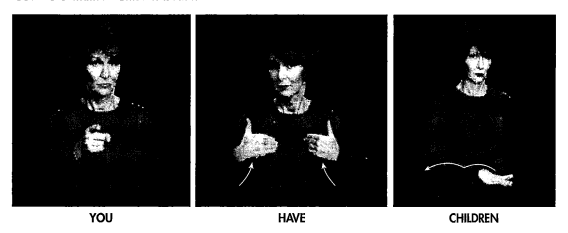

YOU   HAVE   CHILDREN

English: One son.
CS: ONE SON.

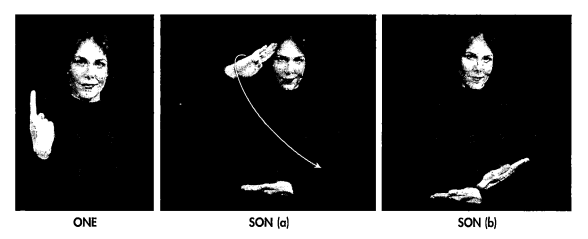

ONE   SON (a)   SON (b)

Additional/Interchangeable Signs

FAMILY, GRANDFATHER, GRANDMOTHER, BROTHER, SISTER, WIFE, DAUGHTER, UNCLE, AUNT, NEPHEW, NIECE, COUSIN, CHILD

FAMILY

GRANDFATHER

GRANDMOTHER

BROTHER

SISTER

WIFE

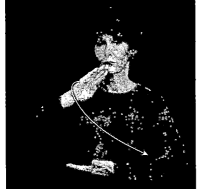

DAUGHTER (a)

DAUGHTER (b)

UNCLE

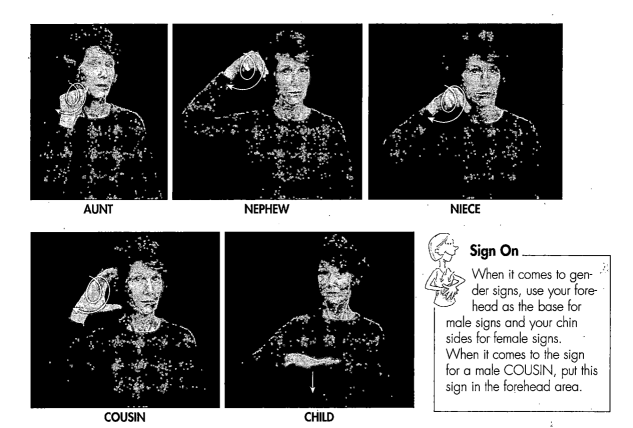

AUNT NEPHEW NIECE

COUSIN CHILD

Sign On

When it comes to gender signs, use your forehead as the base for male signs and your chin sides for female signs. When it comes to the sign for a male COUSIN, put this sign in the forehead area.

Fingerspelled Words

Fingerspell E-X for ex-wife/husband or ex-girlfriend/boyfriend, A-L-L for all.

Personal Stories from CODAs and Their Parents

Children of deaf adults (known as CODAs) have unique experiences growing up living in both the deaf and hearing worlds. They may find themselves pressured trying to fulfill social and cultural expectations from both communities.

Co-author Dawn writes ...

When I was younger, I was highly fluent in ASL because it was my first language. My grandparents (who are hearing), lived across the street from us and taught my brother and me how to vocally form English words and sentences. We also picked up English speech from listening to voices on the radio and television. I knew that I had a great responsibility at a young age. I interpreted a lot for my parents whenever we went out—whether to the doctors, grocery store, gas station, church, or in social gatherings. I was very protective of my parents growing up (and even today!). Sometimes I would get into fights with the kids at school when they made fun of my parents' voices, or when they would run behind my parents and shout mean and hurtful things.

Sign On

CODA, Inc. (Children of Deaf Adults) and KODA (Kids of Deaf Adults) are nonprofit organizations established to promote family awareness and to help children of deaf parents through the dual-identity process. These organizations are open to all those children who have a deaf parent(s), and who may or may not sign.

Sign Off

Do not mock or say words that will be harmful to families and children.

When I became older and started spending my young adult years away from my parents (in an out-of-state university, and in corporate life), I started to lose some of my strength in ASL because I wrote and spoke English all the time with friends and colleagues—It's just such a different communication mode! I missed the range and depth of emotions and expressions that are so embedded in a Deaf home and not so valued in the hearing world. When I introduced hearing people to my parents, I would have to do some preparation first to educate them about how to communicate with my parents. This was always an interesting experience, as some people would clam up and others would be open and outgoing—You'd never know how it would play out until they met face-to-face! It's always my goal to make all people feel comfortable in a communication setting, so sometimes there would be more "damage control" needed to prevent an awkward situation for anyone.

Today, I remain sensitive to the challenges and issues my parents face, and remain in contact with them as much as possible. I know that having communication with others is important to their lives and I hate to think that they feel isolated or left out. We live in the same state, but because it is a distance away, I also rely on e-mails, the TTY, and relay calls to communicate. My husband Mark learned sign language to communicate with my parents, as have some of his family members. Mark and I look forward to having a child and teaching our baby to be bilingual so that he or she will be able to speak to the hearing grandparents and sign to the deaf grandparents. We have a multicultural home and it's a beautiful, rewarding experience.
Dawn's brother Paul states...

My first memory of the question "What is it like to grow up with deaf parents?" occurred when I was in third grade. I was sitting through a geography lesson about the Western United States, when some students from another class asked my teacher if I could come join a discussion they were having about handicapped people. Handicapped people? I gasped! My parents! It did not make any sense; why would my parents interest anyone?

Despite my objections, I was ushered down the hall and quickly found myself addressing 20 or so eight-year olds in front of the blackboard—a typically uncomfortable position for me. This is the last time I wear this shirt: "Prevent Noise Pollution, Use Sign language," I thought to myself. After all, the last thing an eight-year old wants to publicly announce is that he is different. With the spotlight on me, I calmly explained that despite a few lights that flicker when someone rings the doorbell, my life was completely normal and ordinary. Deep down inside, however, I knew it was not.

Admittedly, I was not able to figure out the answer to this question for myself until I was much older and had seen what it was like for others to grow up. I found that I related best to kids that were first-generation Americans, since they tended to have more responsibility at home and faced similar cross-cultural issues. I also found that I was not only a son, but also an instrument, to project the voice and to act as the ears of my parents. The responsibility bestowed upon us to be the voice of the family required my sister and me to assume more mature roles at a young age.

As a teen, the natural internal struggle to become an independent person conflicted with the responsibility I had to my parents to be their instrument. Rebellion, therefore, did not come in the form of tattoos, smoking, or body piercing, but rather in the refusal to interpret for my parents. I used this venue to assert my own independence, and controlled the communication between my parents and the outside world. Gratefully, timely advances in technology provided freedom not only for my parents, but also for me.

Sign On _____

CODAs grow up to work in the field of Deaf education (mostly as interpreters or teachers), or in fields that have nothing to do with deafness. Dr. Donald N. Langenberg earned a doctorate in physics and became the Chancellor of the University of Maryland system, which educates over 130,000 students. Louise Fletcher was born to a deaf minister and became a famous actress, winning an Oscar for Best Actress in 1975 for _One Flew Over the Cuckoo's Nest._ Lon Chaney, whose father was a deaf barber, became a silent film star in movies such as the _Hunchback of Notre Dame_ (1923) and _Phantom of the Opera_ (1925).

We have always been a gadget family. My parents were especially "geeky," highly in tune to the latest in communication achievements. According to our household, the greatest human inventions are the TTY (we had a room in the house dedicated to it), televisions with close captions, wireless pagers, e-mail, instant messenger, Global Positioning System (GPS) devices, and the Internet. Although some of these marvels have been accused of dehumanizing communication between individuals, my experience has been the opposite. Through these technologies, I have seen my parents gain access to things that many take for granted, such as buying airline tickets, arranging for doctor's appointments, and talking with their friends and family.

Our family has always been interesting for others. We speak with our hands and never with our mouths full. Our faces and gestures are quite animated and we make a tremendous impact in a crowded restaurant. My sister and I continue to be instruments for our parents, as we use our voices to speak for them. We still cannot help but occasionally add our own thoughts to the conversation—interrupting and giving our opinions as if we were rebellious teenagers. How marvelous and mysterious this must seem to the passer-by as we intensely kwack type away at a keyboard or talk with feverously dancing hands. But, like I explained when I was in third grade, we are really just a completely normal and ordinary family.

Sign On _____

Be sensitive to bilingual families, and especially to Deaf families.

From the parents of Dawn and Paul, co-author Carole, and her husband, Andy …

Dawn and Paul are our precious and dear gems. We were elated to have two babies, and worked extremely hard to provide the best upbringing environment and experience. We made sure that our children had exposure to both worlds and provided opportunities for well-rounded and healthy social and recreational development. To ensure quality education, we worked several jobs to put our children through private schools and universities. We even put in the same amount of effort to expose Dawn and Paul to diversity and to world traveling. What has hurt us the most over the years of childrearing was the hearing society—hearing educators and hearing family members. They shut us out and instilled negativities on our ability to provide the best for our children. It is our hope that hearing society and family members will become more sensitive with their attitude, words, and approach toward people of difference, and let us experience a happy bilingual family life.

The Least You Need to Know

- ◆ Be sensitive to the diverse experiences of families where there are deaf children of hearing parents, or hearing children of deaf parents.
- ◆ Remember that male-gender signs are located around the forehead region, and female-gender signs are located around the chin or mouth areas.
- ◆ CODA and KODA are two organizations that provide support to children of deaf parents and their families.
- ◆ You now know the signs for members in your family circle!

In This Chapter

◆ Can deaf and hearing people have deep friendships or intimate relationships?

◆ Friendship signs

◆ Making friends in the Deaf community

◆ Signing dinners

Chapter14

Friends and More!

We all need to have friends. We can't change who our family members are, but we do have the option of selecting our friends. We look for people who let us be free to be ourselves when we're around them. Our friends are there to celebrate our successes with us and cheer us up when we're feeling down. They are the ones we can confide in and express our joys and sorrows to. They talk things over with us and give us advice and support to help us get back on track when we lose our way.

Sometimes a friendship can develop into something more—a close or intimate relationship. There's a lot of good in that, too. So, let's be friends!

Can We Be Friends?

In the Deaf community, social bonds and friendships among each other are strong, even moreso than ties to hearing relatives—especially if the hearing family members do not sign. As a minority group in the hearing-majority world, the Deaf community is smaller than the hearing community. Deaf people build deep friendships in their community as they "stick together" and help each other through life's challenges (most have faced multiple experiences of discrimination and oppression). Their strong bonds also develop as they share their common experiences of deafness (positive, negative, and everything in between).

Deaf people place an emphasis on relationships, and invest time and give of themselves to grow and develop the bond. Deaf people will pick up on insincerity and will avoid a friendship with someone whom they feel cannot be trusted—They're good at reading facial expressions and body language, such as when a person avoids eye contact or fidgets restlessly.

Sign Post

The Deaf Community is a close-knit community, and is a strong networking system. Deaf people have many deaf friends. They are rich in diversity, consisting of all ages, colors, gay and straight, rich and poor. For some well-traveled deaf people, this bond of friendship goes beyond their home area to regional, state, and international levels.

Can hearing people and deaf people be friends (or, more than just friends)? There are a lot of views on this controversial topic! Here are some perspectives and insights we've collected from hearing and deaf people on whether or not hearing/deaf relationships can really work at a deep level.

The following do not work:

◆ "It doesn't work if a hearing person acts paternalistic. This is seen when a hearing person makes decisions for deaf people, 'speaks' for deaf people, and takes over situations for deaf people. It makes the relationship unequal—One person becomes like a caretaker or a parent over the other."

◆ "I'm more comfortable with others in the Deaf community. I can express my feelings more, am able to sign, and don't have to stop and repeat myself."

◆ "There are great cultural and language differences between Deaf and hearing communities. Friendships and bonds are easily formed for deaf/hearing signers, deaf/deaf signers, and hearing nonsigners/hearing nonsigners than they are for deaf/hearing nonsigners."

Sign Off

Painstaking confrontations and going through life struggles are common among deaf people in the hearing society. The basic causes are derived from hearing people not knowing and not being aware of the differences in communication ways. As this is a hearing society, deaf people tend to be brushed aside and excluded. Some deaf people have been excluded, abandoned, and punished from activities just because they do not have the ability to hear speech sounds or to communicate through the use of voice. Be sensitive to what is offensive and what is supportive to deaf people. Learn from them through signed communication.

◆ "Deaf people have to make more of an effort to communicate with hearing people than vice-versa."

◆ "I am deaf, but my friend is hearing. Issues arise when we go out with other friends. When we're with either his hearing friends (who don't sign) or my deaf friends (who only sign), eventually one of us feels ignored by the larger group because we can't keep up with what they're saying. Both sets of friends seem to get mad if they have to repeat or explain things to us—Communication is a big problem."

Sign Off

People who are not willing or who do not make an attempt to cross the communication barrier lines thwart opportunities for friendships as well as social relationships.

The following can work:

◆ "Communication is key to any relationship. If a hearing person does not know sign language, it is unlikely that the relationship will survive on a long-term basis. The hearing community uses English, and the Deaf community uses ASL. If both parties are willing to meet each other halfway, if they compromise and use a method to communicate with each other (for example, CS), then the relationship could work."

◆ "It is important to establish rules about when you will interpret for each other when around other deaf friends or hearing nonsigners."

◆ "Learn about each other's cultures and languages. As a hearing person, I got involved in the Deaf community and learned more about deafness. I know that I will never truly know my deaf friend until I can sign as well. To me, pursuing and exploring our differences will bring us closer together. Without that, there is literally just silence between us."

◆ "Be patient. It takes an investment of time to develop a relationship with each other through sign language, which can last a lifetime!"

◆ "Spend fun time with other deaf/hearing couples, or with hearing signers. Find a common ground for things that you both like such as hobbies, fun activities, and topics that you like to discuss."

◆ "Respect each other's communication needs. If I want to be with my hearing friends, my partner allows me to be with them, and visa versa with my partner's deaf friends."

Whether or not a relationship works depends on the two people involved. Every person is different (no two people on Earth are exactly the same) and has different things to bring to the relationship. Like any relationship between two people, we must learn from and accept each other and appreciate each other's differences. As long as both partners communicate well, respect and trust each other, and find a reasonably balanced way of dealing with the world so neither person gets the "short end of the stick," there's no reason why deaf and hearing people can't have great friendships. "Disabilities" and "abilities" aside, the most important thing is to fully accept the person and communicate!

Sign Post

The Deaf community is a supportive community and is sensitive to oppression, discrimination, and negativities. Yet, you will be marveled at their openness and acceptance once you sign! With positive attitude and energy, you will be embraced into this community.

Key Conversational Signs

English: Who is that man?
CS: WHO THAT MAN?

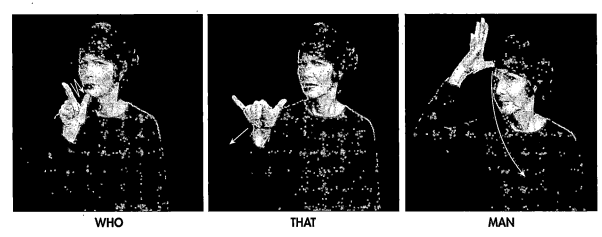

WHO   THAT   MAN

English: My best friend.
CS: MY BEST-FRIEND.

MY   BEST-FRIEND

English: Do you love him?
CS: YOU LOVE HIM?

YOU LOVE HIM

English: Yes. He is so cute.
CS: YES. HE CUTE.

YES HE CUTE

Additional/Interchangeable Signs

BOY, GIRL, WOMAN, FRIEND, PERSON, PEOPLE, LOOK
(APPEARANCE), SAME, DIFFERENT

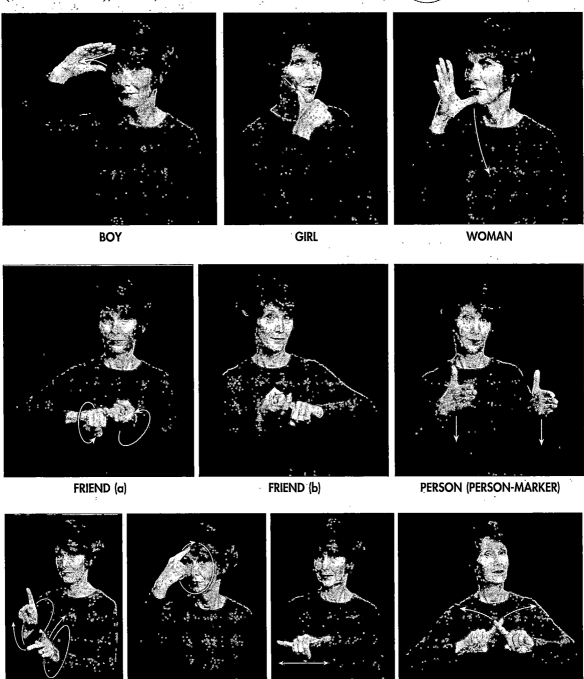

| BOY | GIRL | WOMAN |

| FRIEND (a) | FRIEND (b) | PERSON (PERSON-MARKER) |

| PEOPLE | LOOK (APPEARANCE) | SAME | DIFFERENT |

Sign On

A person-marker (PM) is used in two different ways:

1. To indicate a person's profession. This is equivalent to adding an "-ER" ending to an English infinite verb form, which creates a noun associated with professions. E.g., sign TEACH + PM to express TEACHER; sign WORK + PM to express WORKER.

2. To describe a person's demeanor or attribute. First you sign the PM and then add a descriptive. For example, sign PM and then CUTE to convey a PERSON IS CUTE. Sign PM and then SWEET to express a PERSON IS SWEET.

Fingerspelled Words

Fingerspell C-O-O-L for cool/neat (when emphasized), W-O-W for wow (when emphasized), H-A H-A for haha.

The Latest Way to Make New Deaf Friends

What's the social trend in bringing both hearing and deaf people together? They're called "signing dinners" or "silent suppers."

A signing dinner is a social event where a group meets for dinner either at a local restaurant or at someone's home. The group may have both deaf people and hearing people, or only deaf people. It's a silent supper, as people use their hands instead of their voices to communicate. This is a great way for learning signers to practice their signs in a relaxed setting, make new friends, meet a potential significant other, or just socialize and get to know people in the Deaf community.

Sign Post

When selecting a table, round tables are best, as they enable people to see each other more clearly. If the restaurant allows, you may want to put several tables together to encourage more interaction among the dinner guests.

Try to select the dinner location at a place that is accessible for all—even for those who may not have cars and need to take public transportation. Allow for ample conversation time for this social event—Some people will enjoy chatting for three to four hours. Make sure the restaurant is aware of this, too, so that you aren't rushed out. And enjoy the dinner—through signing, you can share life stories, experiences, feelings, and aspirations. Learn from one another!

The Least You Need to Know

- ◆ We all need friends to share life's experiences with!
- ◆ Deaf people belong to a close-knit community and value friendship, diversity, and long-lasting relationships.
- ◆ Communication, trust, and respect are key to developing a long-term relationship.
- ◆ Signing dinners bring both hearing signers and deaf people together to enjoy supper and to develop social relationships.

In This Part

Part 5

Getting to Know More About You

You're doing terrific! Now you are ready to have more in-depth conversations with deaf people. These next chapters will teach you signs for communicating in everyday life situations whether you're at a party, work, school, visiting someone's home, in a restaurant, or out shopping.

There's a lot ahead, so you can really add to your sign vocabulary and have new options for what to sign. Let's go.

In This Chapter

- ◆ The cycle of life
- ◆ Signs for weddings, births, and funerals
- ◆ Sharing happiness in celebratory occasions and showing support in sorrowful scenarios

Chapter 15

New Beginnings and Endings

We're born, we live, and perhaps marry and give birth to new life, and then we die. That's the reality of our mortal lives. Each of these events—weddings, birth deliveries, and funerals—call for being with others for celebration or support. Deaf people experience all these things along with hearing people as we share an emotion (whether happiness or grief).

In this chapter, you learn signs for these very occasions, known as the best of times and the worst of times in one's life.

Weddings

These conversation scenarios may take place at the wedding ceremony or reception. The typical conversation focuses on love and happiness for the bride and groom, a reflection of the ceremony's events, and people congregating, and having a good time together.

Key Conversational Signs

English: The wedding was wonderful.
CS: WEDDING WONDERFUL.

WEDDING (a)

WEDDING (b)

WONDERFUL

Sign On

The movement of the sign WONDER-FUL begins at the top of the signing space and then ends at the bottom of the signing space. A single movement sign at the top of the signing space is the sign GREAT.

English: The bride and groom are leaving the church.
CS: BRIDE GROOM LEAVE-FROM CHURCH.

BRIDE	GROOM (a)	GROOM (b)
LEAVE-FROM (a)	LEAVE-FROM (b)	CHURCH

English: Follow them to the
reception.
CS: FOLLOW-THEM
RECEPTION.

FOLLOW-THEM	RECEPTION

Additional/Interchangeable Signs

MARRY, KISS, RING, TEMPLE

ON THE
DVD

| MARRY | KISS | RING | TEMPLE |

Fingerspelled Words

Fingerspell H-A-L-L for hall, H-O-T-E-L for
hotel, M-O-T-E-L for motel, I-N-N for inn,
B-B for a bed-and-breakfast inn, and G-I-F-T
for gift.

What You'll Find at Deaf Weddings

At wedding festivities, deaf people may dance as
they feel the vibrations of the sounds, hear the
beat of music, or copy other people's dancing
rhythm and styles. You may even find some
deaf people signing while dancing and even
singing in sign language!

At most deaf weddings, you will observe deaf
people and hearing signers and nonsigners cele-
brating the unity of the couple. Generally, a
hearing clergy or rabbi conducts the wedding
ceremony along with one or two sign-language
interpreters. However, more deaf people are
now becoming ministers, pastors, priests, and
rabbis and may officiate at such weddings. Additionally, there may be deaf and/or hearing
signers who perform parts of the wedding ceremony as poems, readings, and music are signed.

A deaf photographer and/or videographer may
be hired to record the event. When the deaf
couple sign their vows, an interpreter will voice
this so that the hearing audience can hear the
words being signed. Deaf couples tend to provide opportunities for full-accessibility and participation for everyone as this is a very special
moment and time of their lives.

Sign Post

Instead of clapping to show
applause, deaf people may wave
their hands over their heads in the air.

Rabbi Fred Friedman, who is deaf, officiates
Jewish deaf weddings. When hearing people
are present, Rabbi Friedman works with a
hearing Rabbi so that the Ketubah (Jewish
marriage contract) is read in Aramaic while he
simultaneously signs to the deaf couple. Rabbi
Friedman also ensures that the deaf couple
understands the proceedings during the Jewish
wedding ceremony under the chuppah (wedding canopy) so that they can carry out their
mitzvahs (deeds) properly according to Jewish
Law.

Births

Conversations around the birth of a baby often take place at a person's home, in a hospital, or anytime you see someone who obviously appears to be pregnant. When referring to a woman's pregnancy, it is acceptable in the Deaf culture to point to her belly to refer to the baby.

Sign Post

Deaf people are known to be excellent parents and want to raise their hearing children like everyone else. Accept and embrace families of differences!

Key Conversational Signs

English: Surprised that you are pregnant!
CS: SURPRISE YOU PREGNANT!

SURPRISE (a)

SURPRISE (b)

YOU

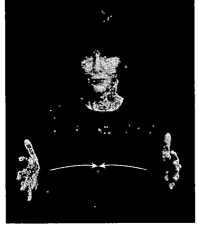

PREGNANT (a)

PREGNANT (b)

English: The baby will be born in four months.
CS: BABY BORN FOUR-MONTHS.

BABY

BORN

FOUR-MONTHS

English: Congratulations!
CS: CONGRATULATIONS!

 Sign Off

Do not feel reserved when it comes to the discussion about pregnancy, birth, and miscarriage. It is a fact of life and is not considered taboo in the Deaf culture.

CONGRATULATIONS

Additional/Interchangeable Signs

EXCITED, NERVOUS, MISCARRY

ON THE
DVD

| EXCITED | NERVOUS | MISCARRY (a) | MISCARRY (b) |

Fingerspelled Words

Fingerspell C-R-I-B for crib, and D-U-E for
due date.

> **Sign On**
>
> The sign for CONGRATULATIONS is
> the same as the sign for MAZEL TOV.
> (Mazel Tov is used by Jewish people to
> mean *congratulations*).

Child-Rearing Education

Carole is an advocate for deaf parents-to-be to
obtain a foundation of childbirth education, as
this has long been considered as one of the
topics for which deaf people lack in-depth
instruction. Historically, sex and childbirth
education are considered taboo, and most hearing parents and teachers who do not have signing skills have not been able to adequately
educate deaf children about the birds and the
bees. A child's birth is critical to her entrance
into the world and to her life development.

Births are to be embraced, with love and joy,
and not be filled with ignorance or the fear of
not knowing what to do. It is a joyful time as it
is the beginning of a new life. Deaf people
need love, positive support, and acceptance
from the hearing society. Child-rearing education is important as it prepares parents for a
child's new beginning. One of life's greatest
gifts is giving—the giving of a positive and
supportive environment to families of differences that surround you.

> **Sign Off**
>
> Be careful not to humiliate deaf peo-
> ple and babies! Ignorance can cause
> humiliation. Refer to Dawn and Paul's
> personal stories (in Chapter 13) about soci-
> ety's treatment toward people of difference
> and the hardships placed on the family by
> people who may not have meant to cause
> harm but inadvertently did cause pain and
> distress.

Deaths

No one likes to talk about death, but it is a part of life and we all experience it through our family, friends, and ourselves at some point. Here are signs that you can use to communicate with a deaf person during this sad time. You may most often use these signs at a funeral parlor or the family's home where you are paying your condolences. The conversation may revolve around the topic of how the person died, how the family (or friends) are doing, and giving your support.

Sign Post ———

At the funeral home, deaf people usually stay for the full time to give support to one another, especially if the deceased person is a member of the Deaf community. An interpreter may be present to facilitate communication between deaf and hearing people.

Key Conversational Signs

English: Sorry that your father died.
CS: SORRY YOUR FATHER DIED.

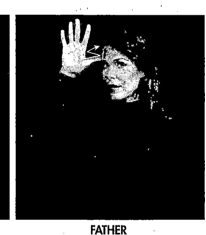

SORRY   YOUR   FATHER

DIED (a)   DIED (b)

English: Thank you for coming to the funeral.
CS: THANK-YOU FOR COME-TO FUNERAL.

THANK-YOU   COME-   FUNERAL

English: The burial service touched my heart.
CS: BURIAL SERVICE TOUCH-HEART.

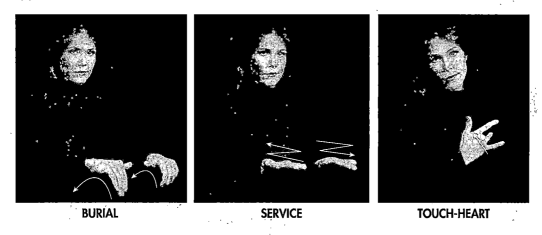

BURIAL   SERVICE   TOUCH-HEART

English: As the priest spoke, I cried.
CS: PRIEST SPEAK (TALK), ME CRY.

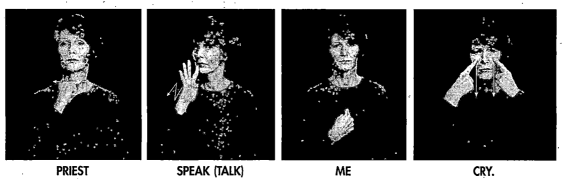

PRIEST   SPEAK (TALK)   ME   CRY.

Additional/Interchangeable Signs

MINISTER, RABBI, SAD

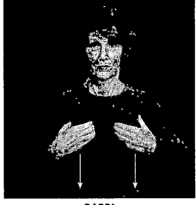

| MINISTER | RABBI | SAD |

Sign Off

It is inconsiderate not to have services interpreted if a deaf person's family member passed away. This person will feel excluded and there may not be an opportunity for the person to experience closure.

Fingerspelled Words

Fingerspell S-O-R-R-Y for sorry (when emphasized), W-H-Y for why, and W-A-K-E for funeral wake.

Hospice Care

Many deaf and hearing people do not accurately understand what hospice is. Hospice is not a "place" but a concept of care designed to provide comfort, dignity, and support to patients and their families when a terminal illness no longer responds to medical treatments. The majority of hospice care is provided in the patient's home, family member's home, or nursing home, although a small percentage

chooses inpatient hospice facilities. Hospice care does not serve to either extend life or accelerate death. It aims to improve the quality of life for a person's last days by addressing the symptoms of the illness and discomfort and pain management; dealing with the emotional, social, and spiritual needs; and by providing bereavement and counseling services to families.

Sign Post

When you visit deaf people who are dying and spending their last days either in the home or at the hospital, be aware and sensitive to their weakening condition. These patients are often very weak so that using their hands or arms may prove to be too exhausting. Given this, these patients may more greatly rely on the use of facial expressions to communicate messages. (Paul J. Daeninck, MD, MSc FRCPC, Director, Palliative Medicine Fellowship Program, Assistant Professor, Dept. of Internal Medicine and Family Medicine, University of Manitoba)

Co-author Carole was recently involved with a committee forming a National Hospice Program for Deaf and Hard-of-Hearing People. Members consisted of both deaf and hearing people representing Canada, Kentucky, Minnesota, and New York. They came together to explore ways to provide services for deaf and hard-of-hearing people facing the last days of their lives. A sensitive issue discussed was that when a deaf person is dying, she may typically be left to die alone without access to communication with hearing family members or health-care members. One of life's most precious gifts would be signing and communicating with a deaf person with love, care, and support before the person departs from the earth. It is extremely distressing and heartbreaking to die alone!

Here is a testimony about Hospice from Paulette Gabel, Deaf Hospice Outreach Coordinator, Jacob Perlow Hospice at Beth Israel Medical Center in New York City:

"Once you discover what hospice is, you see how vital the programs are. Hospice care ensures that patients and their loved ones are not unaccompanied or have unresolved family issues. Deaf patients and their families will face less difficulty while receiving Hospice treatments and comforting care. The patients' values and requests are respected. There are many services provided for the patient and the loved ones such as trained volunteers, social workers, psychologists, nurses, doctors, home-care attendants, personal-care attendants, and a counseling group. They will be there for the patients and their loved ones when needed—especially the sign-language interpreters. The program won't fail to spot anything, knowing what's going on with their ailing loved one, and would never let them feel alone!"

Sign On _____

There are more than 3,000 hospice programs in the United States today. In 1998, these programs cared for nearly 540,000 people.

The Least You Need to Know

◆ Deaf weddings are fun for all—hearing and deaf people alike.

◆ Deaf people, like hearing people, need to learn about sex education, childbirth, and childrearing topics, and to be given the opportunity for in-depth questions and explanations.

◆ Make an effort to spend time communicating with a terminally ill deaf person so she doesn't feel that she is dying alone.

◆ Deaf people who are dying and too weak to use their hands to form signs will rely on the use of facial expressions to communicate.

In This Chapter

- ◆ Being sensitive to deaf people's communication needs
- ◆ Signs for national, religious, and personal holidays
- ◆ Signing Santas
- ◆ It's a party!
- ◆ Sign games to play

Chapter **16**

Special Occasions

Whether you celebrate Christmas, Rosh Hashanah, Kwanzaa, or the like, the United States is a cornucopia for all religious holidays. As Americans, we celebrate national holidays together. During many holidays, the workplace is closed so that people have time to spend with their families and loved ones. Holidays are very often celebrated in one's home, a close friend's home, or in a special gathering place.

It is also an American custom to celebrate the individual—you! Birthdays are an enjoyable excuse for a bash—You're not just getting older, but wiser, too. So kick up your feet and raise your glass as we toast to learning some party signs.

Special Days

Holidays are a time for celebration! Whether we're gift-giving, singing, dancing, eating, and drinking, we're having fun! Special occasions give us a break from the workplace so that we can socialize with family and friends and enjoy their company. It's a time to make merry and catch up with each other, take pleasure in the moment, and also talk about future plans.

Sadly, family holiday gatherings may not be so much fun for those who can't hear and don't feel like they're fully participating in the celebration. When around people singing, laughing, and chatting away, deaf people may feel ignored or hurt if they don't understand what's going on. Many deaf people experience this, and become discouraged and angry or sad. Attempts to communicate with those who don't speak the same language can certainly be frustrating and awkward. Deaf children often cry and become upset. As they get older, they may grow to abhor big family gatherings, which were intended to be happy and great celebrations. But the reality is that it's not fun for deaf people to feel that everyone else around them is having a good time as they sit in silence, waiting or hoping that they will have someone to communicate with.

Sign Off _____

Deaf people will feel left out of joyous holiday celebrations if they are around others who don't use sign language, or if they can't speechread what is being said by friends and family.

So, now you'll learn signs to make the holidays even more special by communicating with a deaf person. Get ready to party!

Sign On _____

If you sign PLAN twice with the double movement, the sign will become PRE-PARE or PREPARATION.

Key Conversational Signs

English: What is your plan to celebrate his birthday?
CS: WHAT YOUR PLAN CELEBRATE HIS BIRTHDAY?

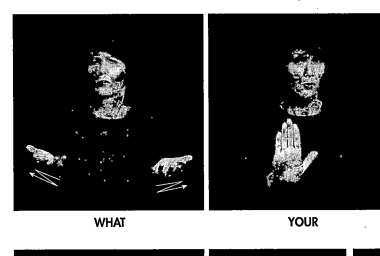

WHAT   YOUR

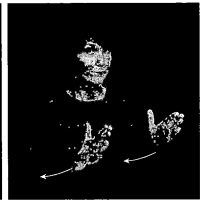

PLAN

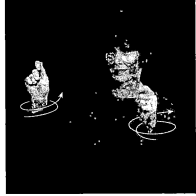

CELEBRATE

HIS

BIRTHDAY

English: A big party. We will dance, chat, have fun.
CS: BIG PARTY. WE WILL DANCE, CHAT, HAVE FUN.

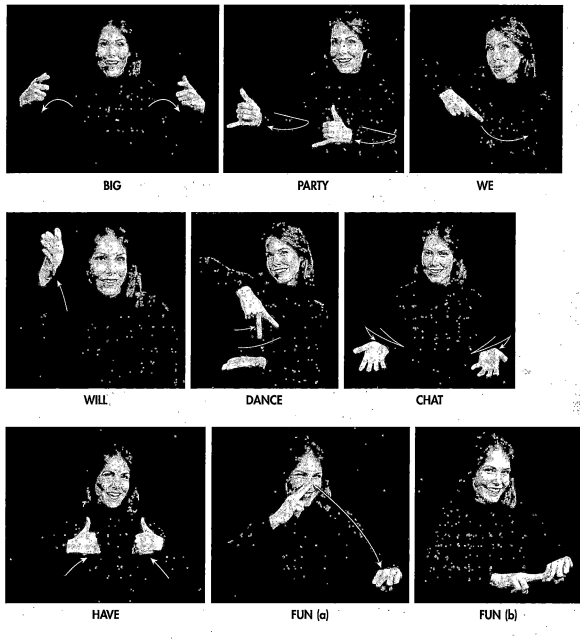

BIG   PARTY   WE

WILL   DANCE   CHAT

HAVE   FUN (a)   FUN (b)

Sign Off

You will see a regional variation of the sign
PARTY. Some will use the Y handshape
and others will use the P handshape.

Additional/Interchangeable Signs

HOLIDAY, VALENTINE, EASTER, PASSOVER, ROSH HASHANAH, HALLOWEEN (PURIM), THANKSGIVING, CHRISTMAS, HANUKAH, KWANZAA, CANDLE, GIFT, SMALL

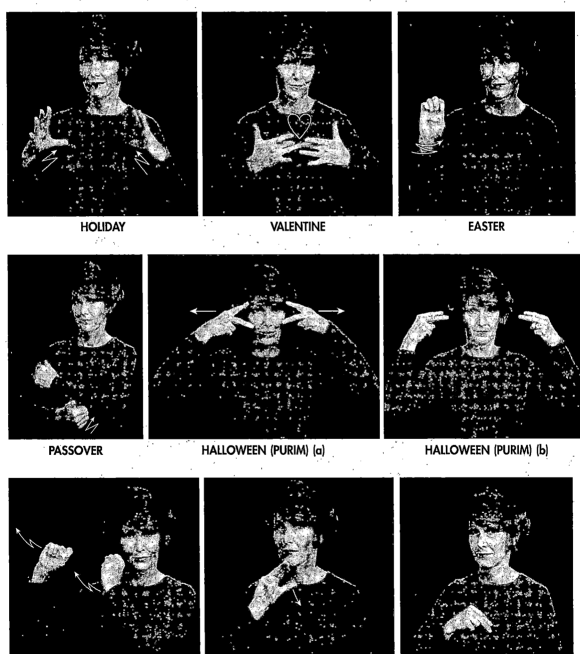

| HOLIDAY | VALENTINE | EASTER |

| PASSOVER | HALLOWEEN (PURIM) (a) | HALLOWEEN (PURIM) (b) |

| ROSH HASHANAH | THANKSGIVING (a) | THANKSGIVING (b) |

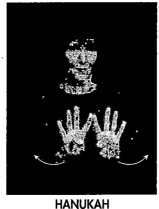

| CHRISTMAS | HANUKAH | KWANZAA |

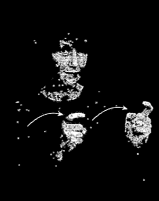

| CANDLE | GIFT | SMALL |

Sign On _____

The sign for HOLIDAY also means VACATION.

Easter may be signed with the movement facing in toward the body or away from the body, depending on local variations.

There are many variations to the signs HAL-LOWEEN (PURIM) and CHRISTMAS across America. The signs shown in the book and DVD are widely used examples; the sign used for HALLOWEEN (PURIM) varies from location to location.

Sign On _____

If you are talking about the width of an object, use the sign you see in the book and DVD for SMALL.

Sign Off _____

You wouldn't use the sign shown for SMALL if you are describing a person. To do this, you would simply gesture the height of the person to imply her short or small size.

Fingerspelled Words

Fingerspell F-U-N for fun (when emphasized) and B-I-G for big (when emphasized).

A Story from a Signing Santa

Some Santas may not shout out a big *ho, ho, ho*, but they can sign it! Outreach programs, schools, and shopping malls across the country may feature a deaf Santa Claus at Christmas time. Just imagine how wonderful it is to see small children, their hands moving so fast that they're a blur, excited to have an opportunity to share with Santa just what gifts they hope to see under their Christmas trees.

Here's a story from a Signing Santa, otherwise known as Eugene Bourquin, Director of Community Services for the Helen Keller National Center for Deaf-Blind Youths and Adults:

"While I was an advanced interpreting student, I was contacted to do an internship that I would never forget! The local shopping mall was having a series of special events for the holiday season, and they needed a Santa Claus who could sign. Reluctantly I took the assignment, but little did I know what joy and happiness it would bring to my spirit.

"On the day that I—oh, I mean Santa—was to arrive from the North Pole, I was quite nervous. Signing is one thing; filling Santa's shoes (and jacket and hat) is quite another. I was escorted to the back of the Christmas village and instructed in Santa Speak 101, what to say, what not to say, and how to *HO, HO, HO*. In my head I quickly tried to imagine how to put these into American Sign Language. I flexed my facial muscles to get the perfect *HO, HO, HO* look.

"Then came the magnificent transformation. I was provided with a considerable tummy addition that increased my weight by a nice 100 pounds. What a physique I displayed. The bright red pants were next, along with the shiny black boots. The jacket handily fit over my new girth, and I started inserting the huge buttons through the fluffy buttonholes. The crowning component of the makeover was a glorious white beard and wig that hid most of my face and flowed down my tummy. A pair of rimmed glasses, a festive cap, and I WAS SANTA!

"I was led to my throne, a grand seat set several feet higher that the floor. I was surrounded by holiday trees, blankets of snow, and strangely motionless reindeer. I waited for my first visitor with knees knocking and hands trembling. Then an angel arrived in the form of an adorable seven-year-old girl. With her mom, she ambled up the path to greet me. I raised my hands and signed a big 'Hello. Merry Christmas!' and the girl's eyes lit up with joy. A look of disbelief passed from her face as she began to sign back a holiday greeting. Mom stood by beaming at the scene. 'So what do YOU want for Christmas …?' began a 10-minute visit for her with Mr. Claus from the North Pole.

"They left and I began to greet the next child, and then the next, and so on, until, in the corner of my eye I noticed waving hands extended from the open floor above me. There she was, my first child and her mom, attempting to get my attention. I waved back and they both smiled. A moment later their hands stilled in the air and they both formed the sign for I LOVE YOU. Santa doesn't usually get too emotional but a tear came to his eye. This was going to be a great day in Santa Land."

Playing "Silent" Games

While Christmas is a popular religious holiday set aside for merriment, it's always great to throw a party and have fun with others whenever you can throughout the year! When you're with a group who's in the mood for

Sign Post

Both hearing and deaf people can be Signing Santas—You just need to be able to sign and understand sign language. There aren't enough of them across the country yet, so maybe you'll want to volunteer one day, too!

playing games, consider some "silent" games so that everyone can participate!

There are many deaf-friendly board games, such as chess, checkers, and Pictionary, and card games such as Uno and Rummy. You can even play bingo knowing some number signs, and use paper and pen to play tic-tac-toe. There are even games that use basic signs, including Sign It! and sign flash cards (such as alphabet, numbers, and basic sign vocabulary).

Here are some ideas for more interactive games:

◆ A variation of the "telephone" game. People stand in a line, facing a wall so they can't see what's going on. One person starts by signing a message to the person next to him, who taps the shoulder of the person next to her and signs the message, and this is repeated to each person in turn down the line. At the end, the last person signs the message for all to see if it was relayed correctly down the line.

◆ A variation of the "fruit basket upset" game. Start with chairs arranged in a circle, one less than the number of people playing. The standing person will try to get to an empty seat as the game progresses. Going around the circle, each person (including the one standing) is alternately given the name of one of three fruits—apple, banana, orange—and shown the sign if he or she doesn't know it. The standing person signs one of these three fruits, and each person sitting in the chairs assigned that fruit name must stand up and then get to another of the now-vacant chairs and sit in it. The standing person also tries to steal a chair. To further throw everyone off, a new standing person may occasionally choose to tumble her hands for "mix up," and then everyone must stand and try to get to an empty chair. If more than 20 people are playing, it is better to have two smaller circles.

> **Sign On**
>
> Remember, whether you play a game or just have a simple conversation, it's great to get all involved (hearing and deaf) so that no one feels excluded and everyone can have a good time.

◆ You can play charades by pantomiming only, so that no talking is allowed. One person mimes things until the other folks correctly guess what it is, such as movie titles (*Gone with the Wind* would be an interesting one!), physical objects (such as a hedge trimmer or football), or actions (such as washing dishes, or riding a bicycle). When pantomiming, you can indicate how many words are in the word or phrase you have in mind by first holding up the appropriate number of fingers. Then, get ready to act silly as people guess what you're trying to mime. The person who guesses correctly gets to be the next up.

◆ It's also fun to teach children the American Manual Alphabet, and have a simple spelling bee (keep it on the easy side and start with three-letter words).

The Least You Need to Know

◆ Be aware to include deaf people in conversations during the holidays—It's supposed to be about "family time," not "alone time."

◆ You learned signs for national, religious, and personal celebrations.

◆ Communicating in sign language is sure to brighten any deaf child's (or adult's) special occasion!

◆ You may wish to add to your celebration by playing games that can promote interaction between deaf and hearing people.

In This Chapter

- ◆ The family dinner table
- ◆ Signs for eating in
- ◆ Signs for eating out
- ◆ Ordering food

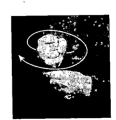

Chapter **17**

It's Time to Eat!

Everybody has to eat! Whether you see food as fuel or food as pleasure, eating is something that we do several times a day. Sometimes we spend a lot of time and effort preparing a great meal. We even have television shows (celebrity chef cooking series on the *Food Channel*), magazines (*Gourmet, Bon Appetit, Saveur*), and classes (Culinary Arts programs) dedicated to our gastronomical pleasures.

And what would Thanksgiving (or any other festive occasion) be without having great goodies to munch on? We each have our secret cravings—chocolate, potato chips, ice cream, pizza, and the like. We may even wait a long time to get seated at our favorite restaurant. Sometimes it's just all about food!

Now we show you signs that you use for food and drinks whether you're at home, on the run and picking up something at a fast-food joint, or savoring a relaxing meal at a restaurant.

I'm Hungry and Thirsty

The kitchen is the heart of the home. Many deaf people prefer to meet, eat, and socialize in the kitchen rather than the living room. The kitchen is where deaf people may have deep conversations about their lives, activities, and issues that they confront daily outside of the home. The kitchen represents the warmth and love of deaf people coming together and talking for hours over a meal.

But in a hearing-majority home, the family dinner table can be a struggle for some deaf children. When others burst out laughing, the child will know that something funny was said, but does not know what. She may feel left out of the enjoyment that others are experiencing. The child may even take it personally and think that others were laughing at her.

Deaf children and adults frequently experience feeling left out from mealtime conversations at a "hearing" table. If hearing people are speaking too quickly, they may forget to wait until the deaf person looks at them before they begin talking. The deaf person's communication needs are disregarded and a lot of information is missed. All too often, when a deaf person asks a hearing person to explain what's going on, they are told, "I'll tell you later," or "You don't need to know this—It's not important."
Unfortunately, the recapturing of "later" usually does not happen. Be aware not to say these two common statements. When deaf people are told "later," you may see them roll their eyes, sign-ing, "Sure, sure," or "Nothing new" with the annoying feeling of oppression and being excluded from the conversation.

Sign Off _____

For a deaf person trying to speech-read someone whose mouth is full is not exactly pleasant to look at!

So, to respect the deaf person and give her a sense of dignity, we'll show you some signs that you can use to communicate with a deaf person at breakfast, lunch, or dinner. These are signs you'll use whether eating in or eating out.

Key Conversational Signs

English: I'm hungry and thirsty.
CS: ME HUNGRY, THIRSTY.

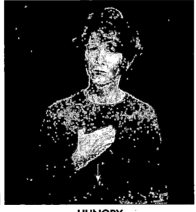

| ME | HUNGRY | THIRSTY |

English: What would you like to eat and drink?
CS: WHAT LIKE EAT, DRINK?

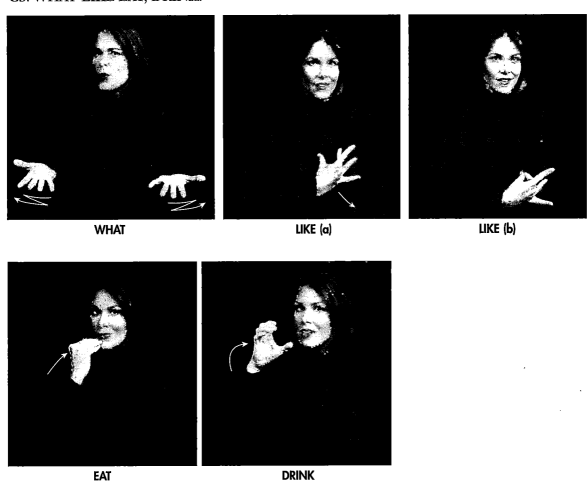

WHAT   LIKE (a)   LIKE (b)

EAT   DRINK

English: I want to go out to a restaurant and order pizza and salad!
CS: WANT GO-OUT RESTAURANT, ORDER PIZZA, SALAD.

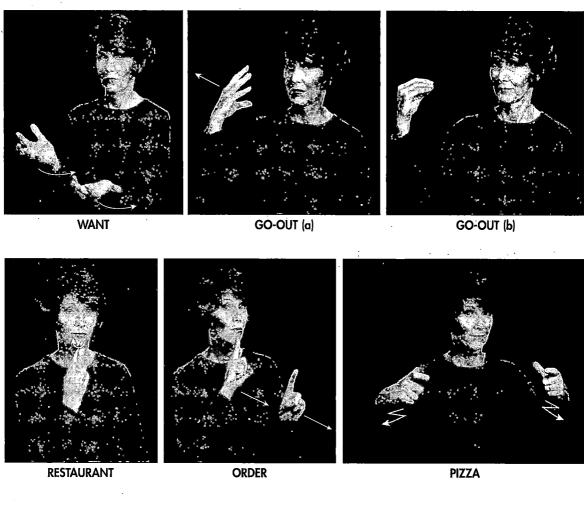

WANT   GO-OUT (a)   GO-OUT (b)

RESTAURANT   ORDER   PIZZA

SALAD

Additional/Interchangeable Signs

HAMBURGER, CHICKEN, MEAT, FISH, SOUP, BREAD, BUTTER, CHEESE, COFFEE, TEA, MILK, WATER, BEER, WINE, COOKIES, ICE-CREAM, PIE, BANANA, APPLE

ON THE DVD

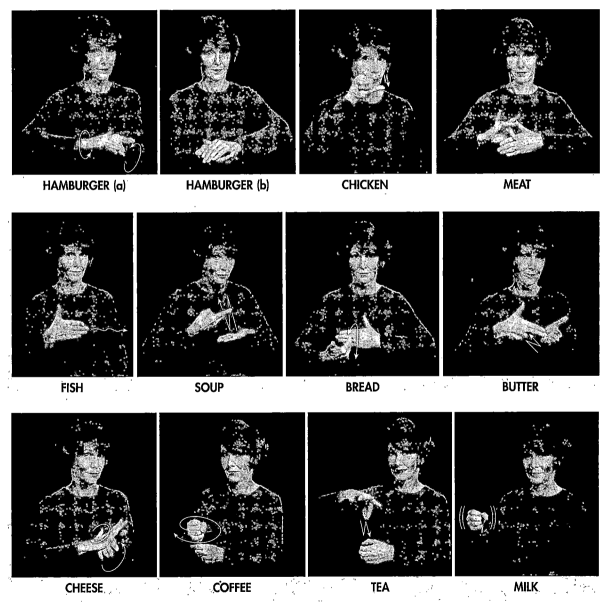

| HAMBURGER (a) | HAMBURGER (b) | CHICKEN | MEAT |

| FISH | SOUP | BREAD | BUTTER |

| CHEESE | COFFEE | TEA | MILK |

Sign On _____

The sign CHICKEN also means bird. Literally, we eat a bird!

Sign On _____

The sign for FISH can imply a fish being dead or alive.

Sign On _____

The sign COFFEE is signed as if you are grinding the coffee in an old-fashioned coffee grinder; the movement is clockwise.

Sign Off _____

Do not sign WINE backward (as commonly misused by new signers). Move this sign clockwise, going forward.

Sign Off _____

Do not sign COFFEE in the movement of twisting your hands back and forth. This will change the meaning to MAK-ING OUT (NECKING). If a deaf person laughs when you make this sign, then you will know why! This happens often in sign-language classes.

Sign On _____

There are many different ways of sign-ing BANANA. Ask a deaf person in your region what sign she uses for BANANA.

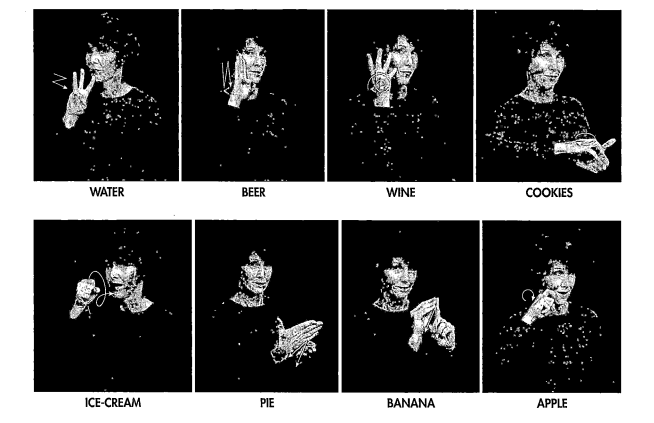

| WATER | BEER | WINE | COOKIES |

| ICE-CREAM | PIE | BANANA | APPLE |

Fingerspelled Words

Fingerspell S-O-D-A for soda, O-J for orange juice, S-A-L-T for salt, and P-E-P-P-E-R for pepper.

Mealtime at a Restaurant

Out at a restaurant? A round table is preferred, as the seating arrangement at the table makes it easier for everyone to see each other clearly. This way, conversations don't need to be interrupted by having to ask someone to change her body position so that her facial expressions and hands can be seen.

When a deaf person orders food visually, it is customary to point to the menu or to the "specials" board if the hearing person (such as a waiter) does not know sign language or is not able to understand gestures. In this case, gestures are typically used to express DRINK, EAT, MENU, and CHECK (BILL).

Typically, deaf people prefer not to order "finger food," such as sticky and greasy chicken that needs to be eaten with the hands. It is rather difficult and annoying to keep wiping or licking your fingers in order to be able to continue with signing. While this may be done at home, it is not the preferred food to eat in public places.

Drive-in fast-food places can be frustrating for deaf people. Hearing people simply drive up to a written post of food items and shout their order into the speaker. Deaf people may drive past the post and have to place their order at the service window by giving a written list of food that they want to order. It can be quite a hassle to have to get out of the car and walk into these places and order food.

Sign Post

In Worcester, South Africa, there is a restaurant located on the school grounds of the De la Bat School for the Deaf. This restaurant is run by deaf people: The waiters are all deaf, the cooks are deaf, and the cashiers are deaf. But most of the customers are hearing; they communicate with the waiters by pointing to the menu! This amazing restaurant is surrounded by glass walls, enabling people to see what is going on outside. In lieu of audial music, there is a visual form of music—a waterfall cascades down one side of the glass walls.

When it comes to ordering food from the home, deaf people typically use the TTY, Video Relay Service, FAX, or the Internet. At first, the hearing person may think a relay call is some kind of prank and may hang up once or several times. Deaf people may connect again to educate the hearing person about the call and begin to order food.

The Least You Need to Know

◆ The kitchen is a place of choice for deaf children and adults to congregate and share discussions.

◆ Be aware of deaf children and adults present who may feel left out from mealtime conversations among hearing people.

◆ Steer clear of sticky finger foods when you know you'll be needing your hands free to sign!

◆ Out at a restaurant, deaf people may use gestures to communicate with hearing wait staff or hostesses.

In This Chapter

- ◆ Home sweet home
- ◆ Inside a Deaf house
- ◆ Signs for indoors and outdoors
- ◆ A future "signing" town

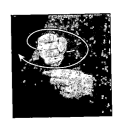

Chapter **18**

My Home and Surroundings

As the phrase goes, "Home is where the heart is." It serves to shelter us from the elements and as a place to keep our personal belongings, but does much more than that. Our home is where we hang out, sleep, eat, dress, and otherwise relax. We entertain guests there, spend quiet time with our families, and sometimes even get to unwind from a hard day in solitude.

In this chapter you learn signs for when you visit a Deaf home—inside the house and out in the yard. So, learn some signs and make yourself at home!

Inside My House

On the outside, a Deaf home may look like any other in the neighborhood. But inside, you'll notice that it has lots of neat gadgets and technologies. You've learned about many of them separately in Chapter 2, but, putting it together now, you may find a TTY (teletypewriter that serves as a phone), television with close captions, and a whole setup of flashing lights— for the TTY, doorbell, and "baby cry" devices. Computers are also used as a communication tool. Other technologies include vibrating devices such as alarm clocks and pagers. As you can see, deaf people have many different options as to how they incorporate visual or vibrating "alert" systems into their homes. Usually, when there are hearing family members present as well, the tendency is to use a combination of light and sound "alert" systems.

So, when you visit a Deaf person's home and ring her doorbell, expect to see lights flashing. Here are some signs you can use to have a conversation once she opens the door to let you in:

Key Conversational Signs

English: Welcome to the house.

CS: WELCOME HOUSE.

WELCOME

HOUSE

Sign On _____

The sign WELCOME has several meanings: WELCOME, YOU ARE WELCOME, and INVITE.

English: Kitchen is beautifully decorated. Where is the bathroom?

CS: KITCHEN BEAUTIFUL DECORATE. WHERE BATHROOM?

KITCHEN

BEAUTIFUL (a)

BEAUTIFUL (b)

DECORATE

WHERE

BATHROOM

English: Upstairs, next to the bedroom.
CS: UPSTAIRS, NEXT BED + ROOM.

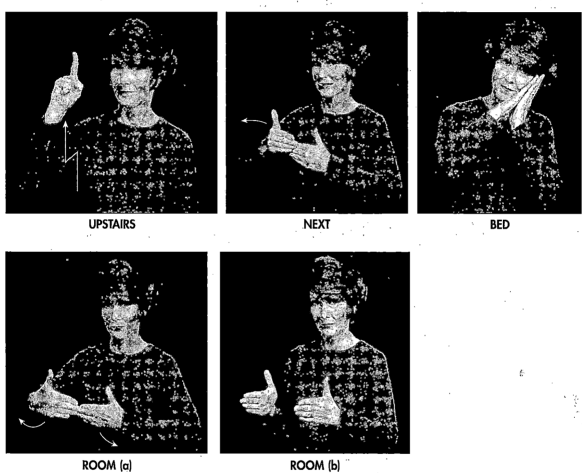

UPSTAIRS   NEXT   BED

ROOM (a)   ROOM (b)

Sign Off _____

If you mean to sign BEDROOM, do not use a long pause between signs BED, ROOM—if you do this it will become two separated items, A BED and A ROOM. Quickly move from one sign to the next to express BEDROOM.

Additional/Interchangeable Signs

DOOR, WINDOW, WALL, FLOOR, TABLE, CHAIR, FURNITURE, BASEMENT, CLEAN, DIRTY, HEAT

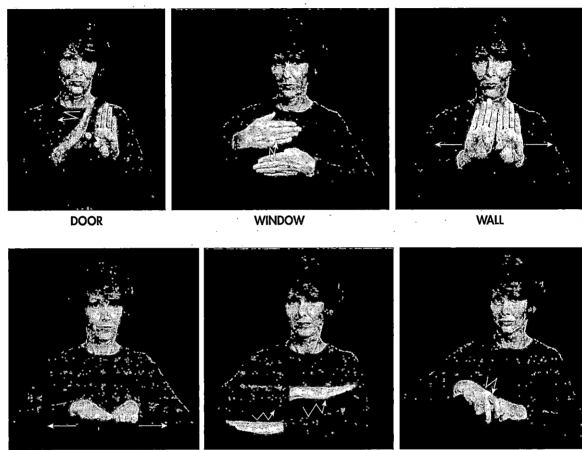

DOOR	WINDOW	WALL

FLOOR	TABLE	CHAIR

> **Sign On**
>
> Signs for DOOR and WINDOW are shown as seen in an average American home. There are variations of this sign according to how the actual door and window would open. For example, the sign shown is for a window that opens and closes horizontally (top to bottom); if you have a window that swings open vertically (from left to right or from right to left), then move your hands in the corresponding direction.

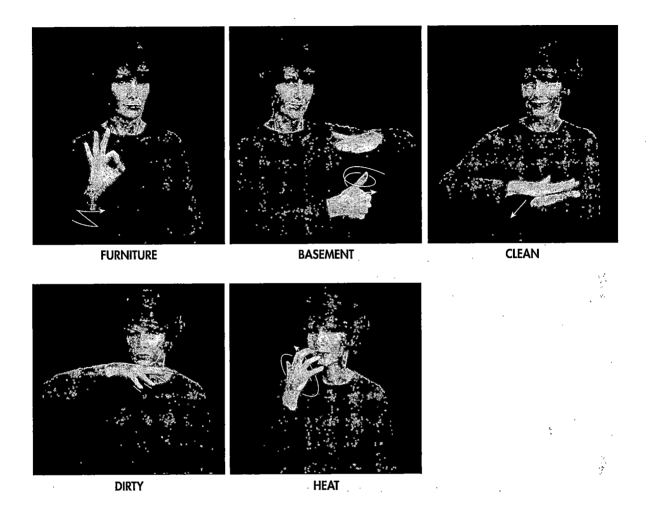

FURNITURE

BASEMENT

CLEAN

DIRTY

HEAT

Fingerspelled Words

Fingerspell A-C for air conditioner, R-U-G for rug or carpet, O-F-F for off, O-N for on, D-U-S-T for dust, G-A-S for gas, and T-V for television.

Assistive Hearing Dogs

Some deaf people may choose to have an assistive-hearing dog in the home, whether living alone or with deaf and hearing family members. These dogs are more than just "pets." The dogs are specially trained to alert deaf people to a variety of household sounds such as an alarm clock, baby cry, smoke alarm, door knock or doorbell, oven buzzer, telephone, or name call. The dogs

are trained so that when they hear a specific sound, they make physical contact with the deaf person and lead her to the source of the sound.

Sign Post

Hearing dogs are identified by an orange collar and leash or vest.

Most centers that train and educate hearing dogs are nonprofit and/or volunteer based. A good resource is Assistance Dogs International (www.adionline.org), which lists hearing dog education centers and assistance dog providers in the United States and internationally.

Many hearing dogs are rescued from shelters, although some are donated by breeders throughout the country. Most are small to medium-sized, and must have the appropriate temperament and personality—energetic, friendly, and people oriented. Many are Golden or Labrador Retrievers or mixed breeds with various combinations of Terrier, Poodle, Cocker, Llasa Apsos, Shih Tzus, and Chihuahuas. It can take up to six months of intensive training until a dog can be certified.

Some deaf people train dogs themselves, and teach signs such as *come*, *go*, *sit*, *stay*, and *stop*. Dogs and other animals have the ability to pick up cues that the person is deaf and will adapt to the person's needs and wishes. Our deaf friend Linda had a cat and trained the cat how to communicate with her. The cat would go up to her and tap her leg when it was hungry. Animals are wonderful resources for alerting deaf people of their surroundings. Even outside of the home, deaf people can look at creatures such as wild birds for sound information—such as when they fly away in a group when a strange animal or person walks by.

Sign Off

While there are some great technological advances that have helped deaf people, there are still more that need to be developed. One deaf couple's water pipe broke and since they were totally unaware of any sounds, the water continued to leak for several months until it poured out from beneath the house. The total bill was over $3,000. They contacted the water company about this situation and applied for their forgiveness program. The bill was reduced to $200.

Key Conversational Signs

Because they are skilled at working with their hands, it is common for deaf people to be handy around the house. They may talk about constructing or rebuilding their homes, or just regular maintenance activities. They may take pleasure in farming and have flower or vegetable gardens. Deaf people may also enjoy socializing with their neighbors, so here are some signs you can learn to chat with your deaf neighbors:

English: Our neighbor is putting in flowers and a tree.
CS: OUR NEIGHBOR PUT-IN FLOWER, TREE

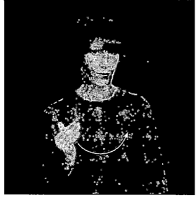 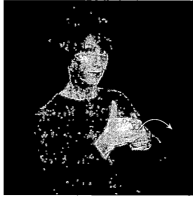 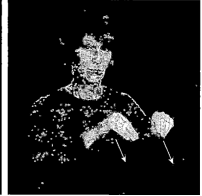

| OUR | NEIGHBOR | PUT-IN |

FLOWER   TREE

English: I need to paint the fence and gate.
CS: NEED PAINT FENCE, GATE.

NEED   PAINT   FENCE

GATE

Sign On

The sign FENCE as shown could be used to express the typical American wooden picket fence. There will be variations to this sign if you have a different kind of fence (for example, solid brick, steel wire rods, or vinyl mesh).

Sign Off

Do not use a sign if it does not match the visual appearance of the object (such as the fence or gate). Use gesture instead, or ask the deaf person how to sign it!

English: Do you want to borrow her paintbrush?
CS: WANT BORROW HER PAINT-BRUSH?

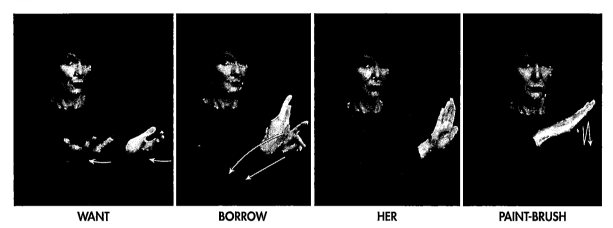

| WANT | BORROW | HER | PAINT-BRUSH |

Additional/Interchangeable Signs

MOW, GRASS, GARBAGE, ANIMAL, DOG, CAT

ON THE
DVD

| MOW | GRASS | GARBAGE | ANIMAL |

| DOG (a) | DOG (b) | CAT |

Sign On _____

There are many variations for the sign DOG in America. The one you see in the book and DVD is the most common sign for DOG.

Fingerspelled Words

Fingerspell P-O-O-L for swimming pool, S-H-E-D for shed, T-O-O-L for tool(s), F-X for fix or repair, R-O-O-F for roof, P-O-L-E for pole, D-G for dog, and C-A-T for cat.

A Town for Signers

In 2005, the United States will have a signing town! Thanks to the vision of Marvin Miller and M.E. Barwacz, Laurent, South Dakota, will be a town where our nation's signing community can gather together to live, work, play, and worship in comfort and beauty. Laurent, SD is not just for deaf or hard-of-hearing people— The town welcomes and embraces hearing people from all walks of life who want to be a part of the sign-language community. It is named after Laurent Clerc, a deaf man who brought sign language to America from France in 1815.

Laurent is not a town built for deaf people. It is a town for people who use sign language. Over two million hearing people in America use sign language—including parents and grandparents of the deaf, children, and siblings of the deaf, and those who hear but have lost or never developed the ability to speak. Additionally, there are individuals who would like to experience a different culture or become fluent in the third most widely used language in the United States. It is important to understand that everyone who wants to travel to or live in a community whose common languages are American Sign Language and written English is welcome to Laurent!

Sign Post _____

Laurent is not a "housing project," but a complete town with one very special element—sign language will be used there. South Dakota's climate provides four seasons, and the area gets over 250 days of sunshine a year. In 1992, *Money Magazine* named Sioux Falls (approximately 35 miles east of Laurent's location), as the number-one best place in America to live.

South Dakota's population is 754,844. Laurent's planned population will be somewhere between 4,000 to 16,000 people. With these numbers, Laurent townspeople can expect to have political influence and an economic impact at both the county and state levels. Laurent will be one of the top-15 largest cities in the state. Very few new communities have the kind of opportunities as Laurent has—easy access to an airport, major medical centers, colleges and universities. Public schools will provide an ASL and English bilingual-bicultural education for all children—deaf, hearing, hard-of-hearing, and those with special needs. By building Laurent as a walkable community and expecting a good public transportation system, parents will not need to be driving children to school or to activities—children will be able to walk, bicycle, or even hop on the trolley!

For more information, visit the website www.laurentsd.com. What a unique and wonderful new home or travel/vacation experience this will be for many. Go!

The Least You Need to Know

◆ Deaf homes have many gadgets and assistive devices.

◆ Hearing dogs are trained to help deaf people by warning them of sounds they need to be attentive to.

◆ You learned signs for things inside or outside your home.

◆ Laurent, South Dakota, will be America's "signing town," opening in 2005.

In This Chapter

- ◆ Making meetings more accessible
- ◆ The ADA and "reasonable accommodations" for deaf employees
- ◆ Signs for the workplace and school
- ◆ A message from the president of Gallaudet

Chapter 19

Work and School

Getting up and going to work and school makes up a big part of our childhood and pre-retirement lives. Sometimes it's just ho-hum and mundane, and sometimes we'll face something that excites or stimulates us. In any event, we spend a large part of our lives trying to get smarter and then putting our acquired skills to use.

Although they say that all work and no play makes one a dull person, finding a balance between work and play isn't easy. Especially in today's world where 9-to-5 jobs are becoming extinct for adults and the school calendar year is becoming longer for children. While this is a reality we all experience, let's be sure to put some fun and interest into our lives and learn some more signs!

Business as Usual

For deaf people, the workplace poses some complicated challenges. They may not have much social interaction with other hearing people, so they may lose out on colleague bonding or learning the unwritten corporate "politics" and nuances that people chat about by the water cooler. There's a lot of talking that takes place that deaf people usually miss out on! Think about all the important messages and other tidbits of information that you hear on the way to work and in the work environment through the course of a day: important news or traffic reports on the radio (including the car radio), voicemail messages, break-room and lunch-room conversations, restroom conversations, cubicle conversations, phone conversations, and meetings. Given all this, deaf people may feel that they are left out of the loop because they lack access to information that hearing people receive.

Clearly, meetings are a frequent method used to communicate and exchange messages in the workplace. Usually when someone calls a meeting, it's to gather everyone together so that they all hear important messages at the same time. Meetings may also be used to solicit participation and perspectives from the group.

Some ideas for what employers can do to make meetings, conferences, and training sessions more deaf friendly include the following:

◆ Provide professional sign-language interpreters or notetakers. They should be booked ahead of the meeting time, and given as much information about the meeting (such as agenda) as possible so that they can adequately prepare.

◆ Arrange chairs in a U-shaped or circular layout so that it's easy to see one another. Ensure that the seating arrangement is also effective for the deaf person to see the interpreter (if present).

◆ Allow only one person to speak at a time.

◆ Point to the person in the audience who is speaking or asking a question and repeat the question before responding.

Sign Post _____

Under the ADA law, an employer is mandated to provide for communication accessibility at the workplace. The employer would need to hire a sign-language interpreter(s) if that is the need of the deaf person. If the meeting lasts for an hour or more, two interpreters should be hired. Interpreters usually work as a team and interpret for approximately 10 to 20 minutes each, depending on the complexity of the topic.

◆ Incorporate visuals such as overhead transparencies, projections from a computer or shown on a large screen, flip-charts, white-boards, or blackboards.

◆ Include captions to describe material presented on overheads or other visual aids, and provide scripts for videos that aren't captioned.

◆ Distribute notes or copies of the presentation.

◆ Begin the meeting by reviewing the agenda, and conclude the meeting by summarizing key points.

Key Conversational Signs

English: An important meeting is being called and the interpreter is ready.
CS: IMPORTANT MEETING CALL, INTERPRETER READY.

IMPORTANT

MEETING (a)

MEETING (b)

| CALL | INTERPRETER | READY |

Sign On

The sign INTERPRETER can be signed in two ways. One way is as shown in the book and DVD (using double-movement of sign) or to sign INTERPRET (using single-movement of sign PERSON-MARKER). Ask a deaf person which sign is used in your area.

Sign On

Depending on your area, READY can be signed as shown (starting with both hands crossed and then using an outward sliding movement) or with two handshape Rs and moving both hands simultaneously in one direction (right to left or left to right, depending on the dominant hand used).

English: I'll stop copying and filing, and go with you.
CS: STOP COPY, FILE, GO-WITH-YOU.

| STOP | COPY (a) | COPY (b) |

FILE   GO-WITH-YOU

English: Hurry! The boss and secretary are waiting.
CS: HURRY! BOSS, SECRETARY WAITING.

HURRY   BOSS

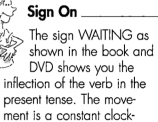

Sign On _____

The sign WAITING as shown in the book and DVD shows you the inflection of the verb in the present tense. The movement is a constant clockwise circle motion.

SECRETARY (a)   SECRETARY (b)   WAITING

Additional/Interchangeable Signs

WORK, COMPUTER, SUPERVISE, MACHINE, BUSY, SIT, STAND

| WORK | COMPUTER | SUPERVISE | MACHINE |

| BUSY | SIT | STAND |

Fingerspelled Words

Fingerspell B-O-S-S for boss, J--B (with B ending faced in toward the body) for job, C-A-S-H for cash,. B-N-K for bank, F-A-X for fax or facsimile, and B-U-S-Y for busy.

Protective Laws in the Workplace

Title I of the Americans with Disabilities Act mandates that employers (employing 15 or more workers) are required to make "reasonable accommodations" in the workplace for the physical or mental limitations of an employee. In general, an accommodation is defined as any change in the work environment or in the way things are customarily done that enables an individual with a disability to have equal employment opportunities.

The National Association of the Deaf (NAD) Law and Advocacy Center (LAC) states that reasonable accommodations for deaf and hard-of-hearing individuals include ...

◆ Telecommunication devices for the deaf (TTYs)

◆ Amplified telephones

◆ Visual alarms

◆ Assistive listening systems

◆ Visible accommodations to communicate audible alarms and messages

◆ Providing interpreter services for employees

NAD LAC indicates that it may be necessary to have interpreter services available on a regular basis for some individuals and some jobs. In addition to their employees, NAD LAC states that employers must ensure that job applicants can communicate effectively when necessary.

> **Sign Post**
>
> In August, 2003, the United Parcel Service (UPS) settled a disabilities-rights class-action suit brought by deaf employees who claimed that the company failed to provide reasonable workplace accommodations (such as its failure and refusal to provide sign-language interpreters for interviews, trainings, staff meetings, and safety sessions) as well as failed to promote deaf workers beyond entry-level or part-time positions. The case was the first employment class-action suit brought on behalf of deaf workers. Filed under the Americans with Disabilities Act, the case awarded $5.8 million in damages for more than 1,000 deaf workers and job applicants.

What an employer needs to do to provide reasonable accommodations depends on the needs of the deaf employee and the nature of the job. Kelby Brick, director of the NAD LAC said, "Employers should always consult with the deaf or hard-of-hearing employee on an individual basis to determine the best way to accommodate the individual."

It's a Student's Life for Me

What is a student's life like for a deaf person? It depends on opportunities available for the person in his or her home area. Co-author Carole shares her story about her experience as a student and later as a professor at a college.

"I began my education at age two and was bused to a school an hour away that had three self-contained classes for deaf and hard-of-hearing children. These classes were oral-based,

as sign language was forbidden at that time in the schools for the deaf. Deaf children who attempted to sign were punished. I then was placed in selected classes with hearing children but without the aid of auxiliary services (years ago, we didn't have notetakers or interpreters in the classrooms). It was difficult to learn subject areas through speechreading without hearing words. I then went onto a hearing high school, once again without auxiliary services. In my third year of high school, I took an entrance examination to Gallaudet University at the age of 16 and was accepted! It was the most remarkable experience getting to meet other deaf people from different parts of America and the world at this all-deaf college. It was at Gallaudet that I learned more about Deaf culture and Deaf identity.

"After graduating from college, I went on for my Masters and Continuing Education certificate program at New York University. At NYU I had sign-language interpreters to interpret the instructor's lessons—a first-time experience. It made a tremendous difference to my learning process in a hearing classroom. This exciting learning experience led me to pursue some courses toward my doctorate at Teachers College, Columbia University. I continue my life-long learning journey and I am a student today, currently taking an online certificate program at Northeastern University.

"I work in the field of education as a faculty member of Human Services at LaGuardia Community College, CUNY. Turning the tables around, I am a deaf teacher who teaches classrooms full of hearing students. In my ASL classes, students are immersed into the Deaf world and I use sign language (and sometimes gestures while they're first learning) to teach and communicate with them. In my Human Services courses I use two sign-language interpreters in the classroom. They take turns voicing my signed lectures to students, and then signing the voiced questions of the students to me. This way of teaching is stimulating and an enriching experience for everyone!"

Key Conversational Signs

English: I like school.
CS: ME LIKE SCHOOL.

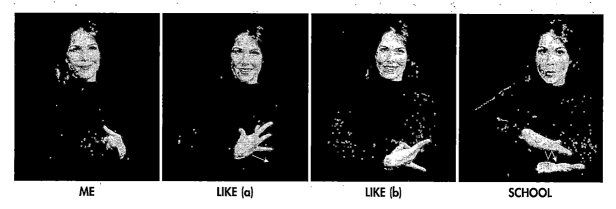

| ME | LIKE (a) | LIKE (b) | SCHOOL |

English: What courses (subjects) are you studying?
CS: WHAT COURSES YOU STUDY?

| WHAT | COURSES | YOU | STUDY |

Sign On _____

The sign COURSES can also be used to mean SUBJECTS and LESSONS.

English: I'm learning math, English, and science.
CS: LEARN MATH, ENGLISH, SCIENCE.

LEARN (a)   LEARN (b)   MATH

ENGLISH   SCIENCE

Additional/Interchangeable Signs

COLLEGE, TEACH, TUTOR, CLASS, BOOK, PAPER, READ, WRITE, CUT (SCISSORS), LISTEN, HISTORY, ART (DRAW), LIBRARY, RIGHT (CORRECT), WRONG (MISTAKE), ASK (QUESTION-TO), ANSWER (REPLY), REMEMBER, FORGET

ON THE DVD

COLLEGE   TEACH   TUTOR   CLASS

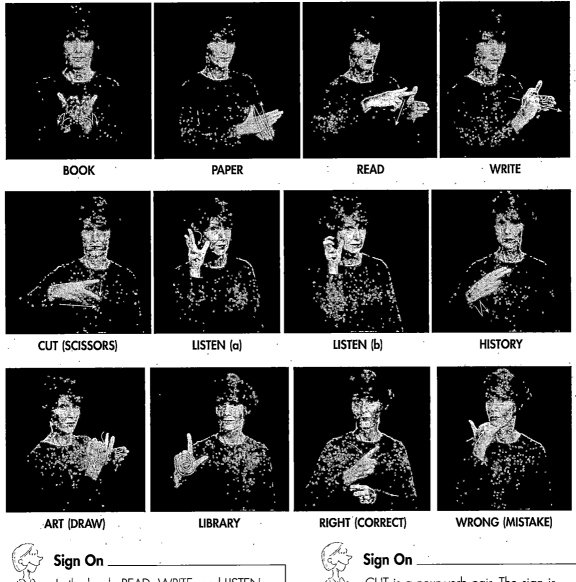

BOOK   PAPER   READ   WRITE

CUT (SCISSORS)   LISTEN (a)   LISTEN (b)   HISTORY

ART (DRAW)   LIBRARY   RIGHT (CORRECT)   WRONG (MISTAKE)

Sign On

In the book, READ, WRITE, and LISTEN are shown with a single movement to indicate the verb and its inflection. In the DVD, the movement is done twice to indicate the present tense of the verb in the "i-n-g" form.

Sign On

CUT is a noun-verb pair. The sign is done once for the verb CUT. If you sign CUT with a double-movement, it changes the meaning to SCISSORS.

Sign Off

Do not confuse the sign RIGHT shown here in the book and DVD to mean the direction (for example, to turn right). This is the sign meaning CORRECT.

ASK (QUESTION-TO) (a)   ASK (QUESTION-TO) (b)   ANSWER (REPLY)

REMEMBER   FORGET (a)   FORGET (b)

Fingerspelled Words

Fingerspell P-E-N for pen, P-E-N-C-I-L for pencil, C-H-A-L-K for chalk, S-U-P-T for superintendent, G-R-A-D-E for grade, H-S for high school, J-H-S for junior high school, and C-C for community college. (Note: If TELEVISION is signed first before C-C, then it changes the meaning to express closed captioned).

Gallaudet University's Message to You

A special message to readers of this book from the President of Gallaudet University, I. King Jordan:

"Hearing people's attitudes about deaf people have changed dramatically during the past 100 years. One hundred years ago, providing educational opportunities to deaf people was considered a "noble undertaking," a "good deed." Not so today. Now deaf people are educated for the same reason that hearing people are—to enable them to grow mentally and socially, and become productive, fulfilled citizens of the nation. With this change in attitude came a dramatic improvement in the level of access to education, employment, and other opportunities.

"Prejudice against deaf people isn't a thing of the past. There are still hearing people who have preconceived notions of what deaf people can't do. They form these opinions based on what their lives would be like if they were deaf. They cannot accept the fact that many deaf people, myself among them, would not choose to take a "magic pill" that would instantly enable them to hear, or that we are totally comfortable with our deafness and regard it as an integral part of who we are as individuals. We have to help these hearing people understand this and get them to focus on all that deaf people can do, instead of what they can't.

"Gallaudet provides deaf and hard-of-hearing students with a high quality and complete educational experience. Gallaudet eliminates the communication frustrations, challenges, and barriers that deafness presents so that students can give their full attention to learning. At Gallaudet, deaf and hard-of-hearing students have none of the communication hassles that they face at other universities. Here they can focus totally on Shakespeare, chemistry, computer science, and other subjects; they can be a trainer for the basketball team or editor of the student newspaper; they can have rap sessions in the cafeteria and argue over the cost of a bag of pretzels with the clerk in the campus store. Gallaudet is the only university in the world where deaf students can do all these things, and many more.

Sign Post

"My advice to all parents of deaf children is to never set limits for your child just because he or she is deaf or hard-of-hearing. Children should be encouraged to dare to dream and to pursue their goals. Help them set high goals and continue to support and encourage them as they prepare for their life's journey."

—I. King Jordan, President, Gallaudet University

"I cannot even begin to list all of the wonderful things I have seen deaf and hard-of-hearing people accomplish during my life. I think the most significant thing I have witnessed is the fact that now we can do anything. We have successful people in all walks of life, whether it is in the corporate world, the education field, the public sector, small businesses, or in the professional arena. When I was a young man, I never heard of a deaf lawyer, and now we have many. Just the other day, I bumped into a young man who said he wanted to become a doctor. I am proud to say that this is becoming more and more common. I have the very best job a deaf individual could have. I feel very fortunate that I am viewed nationally and internationally as a role model and symbol of a successful deaf person."

The Least You Need to Know

◆ Under the Americans with Disabilities Act, an employer must provide for "reasonable accommodation" in the work place.

◆ There are many things you can do to make meetings, conferences, and training sessions more accessible to deaf people.

◆ Don't set limits on deaf children; they deserve the opportunity to receive a great education so that they may grow up to be highly educated and skilled adults.

◆ Keep up the good work! You're a great student!

In This Chapter

◆ Deaf influences in sports practices used today

◆ Signs for participatory and spectator sports

◆ Iconic sports signs

◆ Deaf people in the Olympics

Let's Play Sports

Many of us, male and female, love to play sports. It's lively and it's thrilling; it gives us a charge to yell and cheer for our teams. It gives us a good workout and keeps us competitive when we play sports ourselves.

In this chapter you will learn basic signs for sports you play in a group and individually. There are sports signs to use whether you're actively participating with others, or watching a live or televised game.

You're a Good Sport!

Baseball is one of America's favorite sports. But did you know that a deaf person was responsible for some things that we've come to love about the game? A famous deaf baseball player, William "Dummy" Hoy, played professional baseball for several teams in the major leagues from 1888 to 1902, including the Cincinnati Reds, the Washington Senators, and the Chicago White Sox. Although he was the first player to hit what was termed a "grand slam" in the American League, Hoy's biggest claim to fame is the credit he has received for inventing the hand signals used today by umpires. He asked the umpires to raise their right arm to signify a "strike" and to raise their left arm to signify a "ball." The signals used today in baseball for "out" and "safe" can also be attributed to Hoy.

And he's influenced some baseball signs in sign language, too. Signs for strikes are performed on the right hand, while balls are on the left hand, and the sign for safe is the same as the gesture used in the game.

Sign Post

Hoy was inducted into the Ohio Baseball Hall of Fame. In 1961, he threw out the ceremonial first pitch to open the World Series between the Cincinnati Reds and the New York Yankees at the age of 99. Hoy passed away two months later.

A group of deaf people are also responsible for a great idea that has become imbedded in the sport of football. Star quarterback Paul Hubbard of Gallaudet University's football team (the Bison) invented the football huddle in 1894. Hubbard was worried that other deaf and hearing teams were reading the signed messages he gave his team members and thus intercepting plays. So, he gathered his players in a huddle to keep their sign language private and prevent this "eavesdropping." Other teams liked this idea for secret conversations so much that it was copied and grew in popularity to become a practice used by every football team today.

You'll notice that many sports signs are iconic, meaning that they very closely resemble what it is they're depicting (for example, the sign for GOLF suggests that you're swinging your club; the sign for TENNIS suggests that you are hitting the ball with the racket; the sign for FREESTYLE SWIMMING suggests that you are moving in the same motion used to swim this stroke in the water).

Remember what you learned in Chapter 6 about noun-verb pairs? You'll use this here, too. Some examples are the signs (also iconic!) BASEBALL and FOOTBALL. The sign for BASEBALL is similar to the gesture of swinging a bat: Swing once and it's a verb; swing twice and it's a noun. The same goes for football—the sign of throwing the football from your shoulder. Gesture that it's thrown once and you indicate the verb (playing) FOOTBALL; gesture that it's thrown twice and you're signing (the game) FOOTBALL.

Key Conversational Signs

English: I am watching a football game.
CS: ME WATCH FOOTBALL GAME.

| ME | WATCH | FOOTBALL | GAME |

English: The blue team is playing against the yellow.
CS: BLUE TEAM PLAY AGAINST YELLOW.

BLUE

TEAM

PLAY

AGAINST

YELLOW

English: A touchdown!
CS: TOUCHDOWN!

TOUCHDOWN

Sign On

You can differentiate the score for a team you're rooting for versus a team your friend is rooting for. First sign SCORE, and then sign the score numbers near your body for your team, and sign the score numbers toward the other person for the team he or she is hoping will win. Remember, it's not if you win or lose, but how you play the game!

Additional/Interchangeable Signs

BASEBALL, BASKETBALL, SOCCER, BALL, WINNING, LOSING

BASEBALL

BASKETBALL

SOCCER

BALL

WINNING

LOSING

 Sign On _____

To sign PLAYER, use the two signs PLAY + PERSON-MARKER.

Sign On _____

The signs shown for WINNING and LOSING are common gestural signs as used by sport fans when they come together to watch or root for their team.

Fingerspelled Words

Fingerspell B-A-L-L for ball and also for pitched "ball" call in baseball, S-C-O-R-E for score, and G-A-M-E for game.

Deaf Olympic Athletes

Deaf athletes from around the world practice in their country's training camps along with hearing athletes in the hopes that they will advance on to sport's toughest competition—the Olympics. Deaf people have been competing in the international Olympic Games at least since 1948, when China's Lau Wen-Ngau ran the marathon event. Here are some recent deaf Olympic athletes, along with their home country, sport event, and Olympic game year ...

◆ Terence Parkin, South Africa, Swimming, 2000

Sign Post

Terence Parkin went on to win a silver medal in the 2000 Olympic Games held in Sydney, Australia, for the 200-meter breaststroke event. He is still heavily involved in high-profile swimming competitions today. He competed in the 2003 LC World Championships, coming in fifteenth for his 200 breaststroke event.

◆ Yuri Jaanson, Estonia, Rowing, 1992
◆ Dean Smith, Australia, Decathlon, 1992
◆ Dave Wharton, USA, Swimming, 1988
◆ Frank Martin, Australia, Track, 1984
◆ Pierro Italiano, Italy, Diving, 1984
◆ Jeff Float, USA, Swimming, 1984

As you can see, the Olympic events they participated in are quite varied, proving once again that deaf people can do it, too!

The Least You Need to Know

◆ Deaf people have contributed to the way baseball and football are played in America.
◆ Many sports signs are iconic (meaning that the sign resembles the action it represents).
◆ There are signs for sports of all sorts!
◆ Deaf people compete in the international Olympics.

In This Chapter

- ◆ Spend, spend, spend or save, save, save
- ◆ Signs for shopping and banking needs
- ◆ The almighty dollar

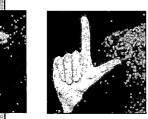

Chapter 21

Shopping and Other Activities

Every day we're tempted by not-so-subtle advertisements showing us lots of ways to spend all our hard-earned money! Televisions, radios, magazines, catalogs, and the internet all blast enticing messages of what our life could be like if only we owned the ABC product or XYZ service they're selling! There are zillions of options as to what these may be! However, the Internet stock-market crash beginning in April 2000 triggered a downward spiral for economies in America and abroad. Since then, working families have struggled. Incomes are flat or down, while job loss, unemployment, health-care costs, poverty, and personal bank-ruptcies are all up. Being thrifty is the name of the game.

In this chapter, you learn signs used for paying your bills and spending your cash. And in today's economy, it makes sense to wisely use your dollars and cents!

Spending My Money!

These days, companies want to make it oh-so-easy for you to spend your money. Don't have enough cash in your wallet or money in the bank? Use a credit or debit card. Too difficult to carry the item that you purchased to your home? It can be shipped to you. Don't have time to go to the store? Hire a personal shopper or fashion consultant. And to do everything all at once without having to speak to another human being, you can shop on the Internet.

The Internet enables you to shop 24 hours a day. On the Internet you can search and find unique items not sold in your hometown, and even have items mailed to you directly from a store in another country. You can also bargain-shop. You can even find companies on the Internet that will ship your purchases for free. Now, that's being thrifty!

Sign Post _____

The Internet is great for comparing the prices of items, and you may find something for less than the sale price from your local store.

Sometimes deaf people may experience difficulty during check-out at the store. They may not be able to speechread the cashier, who generally calls out the price to be paid. This is especially trying if the cashier is looking down while speaking, as they often do when they count money. Also, words such as 50 CENTS and 15 CENTS look very similar to a speechreader. That's not all similar! Deaf people may look to see the total purchase price shown on the cash register. But sometimes display units may block their view of the cash register.

Technology may offer an option here. Across the country, a few stores are piloting the latest method to pay for goods—Automated Checkout Machines (ACMs). From grocery store chains to Home Depot, BJ's Wholesale Club, and Dillion's, some retailers are exploring the possibility of using technology, ultimately replacing the need for human cashiers. Similar to the concept of buying gas and paying at the pump, the ACM enables you to scan the items you wish to purchase, and totals the price and appropriate taxes when completed. You then insert your cash, credit card, or debit card into the ACM to make your payment. A scale, which weighs the items, confirms that your payment is correct (and that you aren't leaving the store with an unpaid item). Some ACMs are programmed to scan coupons and to give a receipt.

Sign Post _____

"I think that the ACMs will take some time to catch on with the general public, but once you start using them I think they are great. It sure got me out of the store quicker."

—Estelle Kircher, after using an Automated Checkout Machine for her groceries

Now we look at some signs that will help as you shop.

Key Conversational Signs

English: I am going shopping with 500 dollars to spend.
CS: ME GO-TO SHOPPING WITH 500 DOLLARS TO-SPEND.

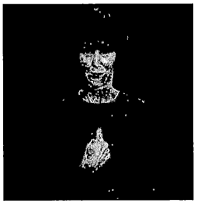

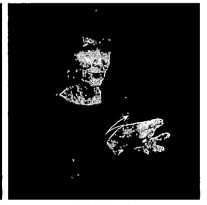

| ME | GO-TO | SHOPPING |

Sign On

Remember the noun-verb pair signs!
The sign SHOPPING is a noun and uses
a double-movement. When a single-
movement is used, it becomes a verb, to BUY.

Sign On

In addition to expressing time, rules
change for the use of the manual number signs when expressing numbers in
the hundreds or thousands, phone numbers,
social security numbers, and credit card numbers. The orientation of the palm for signing
time numbers from 1 to 9 will face outward.

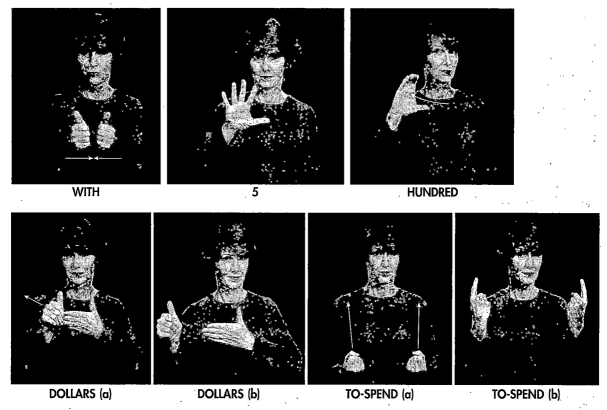

| WITH | 5 | HUNDRED |

| DOLLARS (a) | DOLLARS (b) | TO-SPEND (a) | TO-SPEND (b) |

English: What are you going to
buy?
CS: WHAT BUY?

WHAT   BUY

English: Clothes! Shoes, pants, and a coat.
CS: CLOTHES! SHOES, PANTS, COAT.

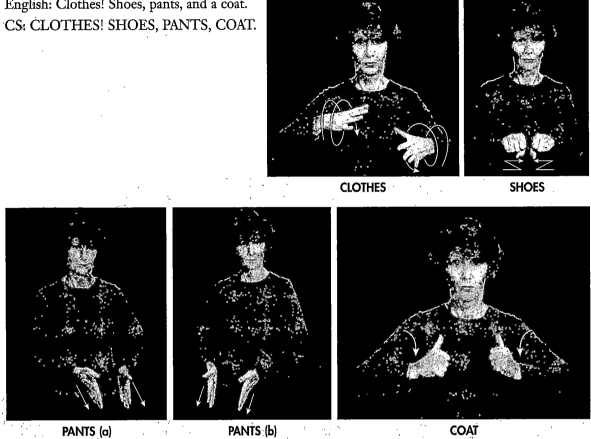

CLOTHES SHOES

PANTS (a) PANTS (b) COAT

English: When you're finished, two of us should watch a movie.
CS: WHEN FINISH (DONE), WE-TWO SHOULD WATCH MOVIE.

WHEN FINISH (DONE) WE-TWO

SHOULD   WATCH   MOVIE

 Sign On

One of the interesting features of sign-ing is that the numerical system is incor-porated into the sign WE-TWO (using two fingers to represent *me and you*). You could also sign WE-THREE (using three fin-gers to represent the *three of us*, moving in a counter-clockwise motion).

 Sign On

In English, when a person asks you what you will buy on your shopping excursion, you answer by mentioning the specific item(s) you plan to purchase. In sign language, we sign the general concept first and then the specific item. For example, if I am going food shopping, I would sign FOOD, MILK, BREAD, COOKIES. If I want to express that I am going to buy a shirt and pants, I would sign CLOTHES, SHIRT, PANTS.

 Sign Off

Be careful not to confuse the signs SHOULD (signed with softer intensity) and NEED (signed with stronger intensity).

Additional/Interchangeable Signs

STORE, SOCKS, SHIRT, SKIRT, SHORTS, EYEGLASSES, MONEY, CENTS, HOW-MUCH, WALK

ON THE DVD

STORE   SOCKS   SHIRT   SKIRT

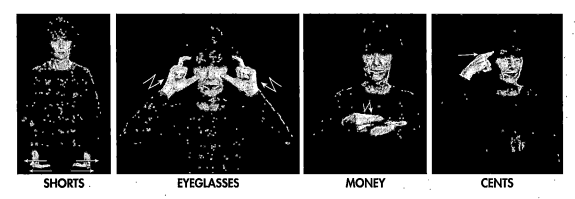

SHORTS   EYEGLASSES   MONEY   CENTS

HOW-MUCH (a)   HOW-MUCH (b)   WALK

 Sign On _____

EYEGLASSES is another noun-verb pair. Remember, a single-movement makes it a verb and the double-movement of the sign changes it to a noun. To express *sunglasses*, you would fingerspell S-U-N and then sign EYEGLASSES.

Fingerspelled Words

Fingerspell S-H-O-P for a shop (store), H-A-T for hat, B-A-G for bag, S-A-L-E for sale, T-A-X for tax, M-A-L-L for shopping mall, T-O-Y for toy, S-I-Z-E for size, Z-O-O for zoo, and P-A-R-K for recreational park area.

Story About a Deaf Philanthropist

There are deaf individuals who use their financial resources to benefit the lives of others. Instead of spending their money on themselves, they choose to contribute their dollars and cents to helping other deaf as well as hearing people.

One such person is Jim Macfadden, a graduate from Gallaudet College, who is deaf and a self-made success story. After graduating from college, he worked for over 10 different computer services firms. Although his great talent was recognized and he was given increased responsibilities, he continually found that his managers did not know how to deal with his deafness. Jim knew that this limited his ability to progress and reach his highest potential. Frustrated, he decided to take the risk and go out on his own after yet another rather ugly experience with a manager.

Twenty-five years later, Jim now owns a company that develops computer software applications and manages several large programs for federal agencies, such as the US State Department, the Food and Drug Administration, Peace Corps, and the Environmental Protection Agency. Jim has often said that a major ingredient to his success has been some of the unpleasant examples of some of his former managers—this taught him very well how *not* to manager other employees. Jim learned from his bad experiences and strived to become a strong, fair, and effective leader and manager. With over 75 employees, his company has been in business for about 18 years, with revenues over $12 million a year.

Jim uses his business success to better the lives of other deaf people. He says, "I have always believed in supporting organizations and institutions that perform valuable services for the Deaf community. With my company being more successful, I simply have been able to increase the amount of support I have provided overall these years." Jim donates to help maintain senior citizen homes; sponsors events that promote disability awareness; spends money to enhance lives of people who desperately need help; and makes contributions to several organizations for better quality services and education such as Gallaudet University, the National Association of the Deaf, and the Maryland Association of the Deaf. These are only a few examples—not to mention how much more he has done! He has been able to improve the lives of deaf people and at the same time, heighten awareness and respect for this unique population.

Jim encourages all people to donate to others. He says, "I look at philanthropy as a social obligation. Everyone should contribute what they can afford to those organizations that have helped them in life and whose causes they support. These organizations need support. $100, $50, or even $25 a year is greatly appreciated by many organizations. Many of these organizations can get money from larger philanthropy organizations simply based upon the number of contributors."

> **Sign Post** _____
>
> There are many deaf people who spend money in philanthropic ways that include research organizations, education institutions, social and event parties, membership in local and national associations, and travels to other states and countries. Others are patrons of the arts, such as galleries, museums, and theaters.

Many deaf people understand the need to further advance deaf awareness programs as well as the need to reach out to necessities within the Deaf community. They may make contributions to their local organizations and clubs as well as directly helping others who are in need. Their donations may not always be money—they may contribute their energy and time, food, clothing articles, talents and skills. It is not uncommon for a deaf person to commute to another deaf person's home to bring food, supplies and other such things. This is a close-knit community and deaf people know the value and personal rewards of spending money to help each other.

The Least You Need to Know

◆ The Internet provides opportunities for deaf people to shop without communication struggles.

◆ Automated Checkout Machines are popping up across the country as an option to enable people to scan in their items for purchase and make payments without having to use a live cashier. This technology creates parity between deaf and hearing consumers.

◆ You learned signs for basic clothes.

◆ You now know signs for shopping, banking, and recreation.

In This Part

Part **6**

Giving a Helping Hand

In this next set of chapters, you learn signs for communicating with deaf people through life's more challenging or problematic circumstances. These signs are beneficial for helping someone who may be lost, sick, or needing to communicate matters regarding law enforcement issues or a fire.

In times of trouble or emergency, you can help to clarify situations that could be otherwise frustrating or terrifying. And so, in advance, thanks for your help!

In This Chapter

- ◆ Hit the road!
- ◆ Technological advances in navigation systems and transportation modes
- ◆ Signs for directions and transport means
- ◆ Ways of moving around

Chapter 22

Where Am I Going and How Do I Get There?

So you're behind the wheel and trying to get to your final destination. Whether it's you or a deaf person who is lost, it's helpful to learn some signs that can point you to where you need to go and what means you should use to get there.

So let's go on the road and learn some signs for direction and transportation.

Directions

Sooner or later, we all get lost in our travels. We may have taken a wrong turn here and there, or just totally misplaced the directions. This may happen when you are in a new location or area and are trying to find the place. This occurs in a city, town, or countryside. You may try to find a gas station or local resident to help you with the directions. Even as a hearing person, you may use gestures (such as pointing) or visual methods (maps, paper-and-pen drawings) as an aid in your communication to figure out where you're going.

Deaf people may keep a map or a notepad in their cars in the anticipation that they may need to get directions visually. When you give visual directions, try to picture the layout of the area with streets and number of stop signs or lights. It is important to be accurate with your visual layout as if you were driving to the site. It is also helpful to add visual landmarks while you give directions. You can draw the layout and explain at the same time by using gestures if you don't know the signs.

Key Conversational Signs

English: I am lost.
CS: ME LOST.

Sign On ——————

If you do not have a map or paper and a pen, use your palm to "draw" imaginary directions on your hand.

| ME | LOST (a) | LOST (b) |

English: Can I help you?
CS: CAN ME-HELP-YOU?

| CAN | ME-HELP-YOU |

English: I'm looking for the highway.
CS: LOOK-FOR HIGHWAY.

Sign On ——————

The sign LOOK-FOR also means SEARCH.

| LOOK-FOR | HIGHWAY |

English: At the light, turn right. After four blocks, go left.
CS: TRAFFIC-LIGHT, GO-RIGHT. AFTER FOUR BLOCKS, GO-LEFT.

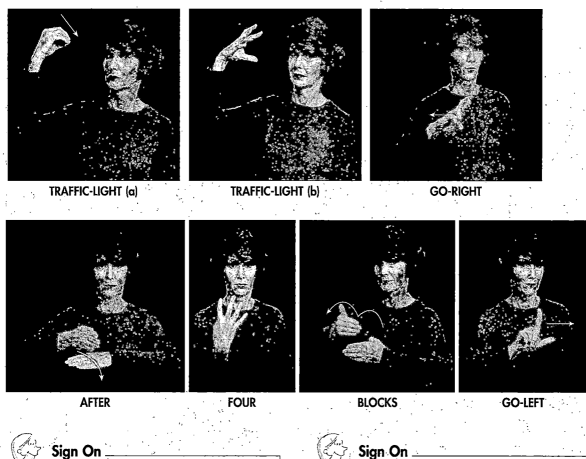

TRAFFIC-LIGHT (a)   TRAFFIC-LIGHT (b)   GO-RIGHT

AFTER   FOUR   BLOCKS   GO-LEFT

Sign On _____
TRAFFIC-LIGHT is also a noun-verb pair.

Sign On _____
There are local variations to the signs GO-RIGHT and GO-LEFT. Some people may use an OPEN B (CLOSED 5) handshape or some may use the number three handshape. Ask a deaf person what is being used in your region.

Additional/Interchangeable Signs

ADDRESS, NORTH, SOUTH, EAST, WEST, BEFORE

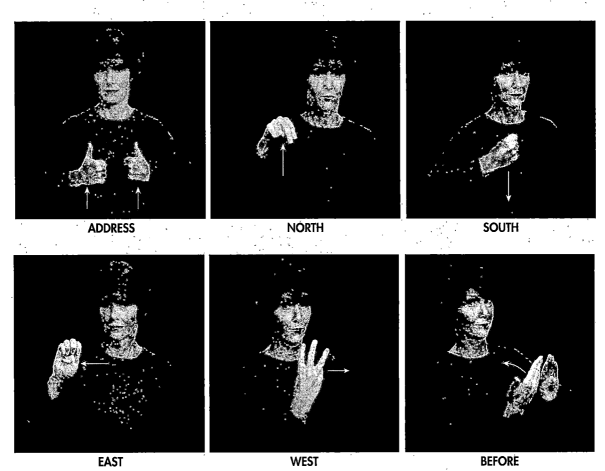

ADDRESS	NORTH	SOUTH
EAST	WEST	BEFORE

Fingerspelled Words

Fingerspell S-T for street, A-V-E for avenue, R-O-A-D for road, M-A-I-N for "Main Street," T-P for turnpike, T-O-L-L for toll, and E-Z for EZ pass used to pay bridges and tolls (used in some states).

Global Positioning Systems

Are you still lost? Advances in visual technology can help you navigate to your destination. Global Positioning Systems (GPS) came out of a $12 billion dollar project from the U.S. Department of Defense who aimed to support the military with a precise form of worldwide positioning tool. Twenty-four satellites were placed in space, supported by ground stations to create a worldwide radio-navigation system. These satellites are so precise that they can calculate positions to a centimeter within range.

Some companies have capitalized on this high-tech equipment sitting in space and have created GPS "receivers" that can be purchased for use by the general public. Due to national security restrictions, the best of the receivers for the public can only calculate positions within nine to ten feet. These receivers are small units that people can use as navigation tools in their cars, boats, planes, and computers (hand-held and laptop). Simply, you can use the GPS by typing in your current and desired location. Then, a screen shows you a map, which guides you with details on how to get from point A to point B. That's where the fun is (and why prices vary on GPS systems), because of the variations found in the visual maps (the level of details and intricacies differ). Some may have special features such as state and country boundaries, lakes, rivers, streams, airports, cities, towns, coastlines, state and interstate highways, local thoroughfares and secondary roads within metro areas, and federal interstate highway exit information for services

such as food and lodging, and truck, RV, and automotive service stations. You can even use some sophisticated GPS systems to query the topography along your route.

For all these benefits, GPS systems are certainly becoming more popular and widespread. Now there's no excuse for getting lost!

Transportation

Deaf people do not let their deafness impede their ability to be excellent drivers, and many may sign and drive at the same time. When you sit next to a deaf driver, you'll notice how she multitasks—signing to you, looking at the rear view mirror and side mirrors, and watching the road at the same time. Be aware that when you are in a car with a deaf driver, she may use one-handed signing. Do not be alarmed if she is "watching" you as she can see out of the corner of the eye and use her peripheral vision. This may not be applicable when it comes to driving along curved roads or road construction; then it may be time to hold on to the conversation. The deaf driver will let you know when it is a good time for you to sign again. When you are sitting in the back seat, the deaf driver may converse with you via using the rear-view mirror.

Key Conversational Signs

English: How do you get to the airport?
CS: HOW YOU GET-TO AIRPORT?

 Sign On _____

The sign GET-TO is also used to express ARRIVE-TO. This can be a directional sign. To do this, first sign the destination at a specified place in your signing space and then sign GET-TO toward the area. For example, sign HOUSE, GET-TO.

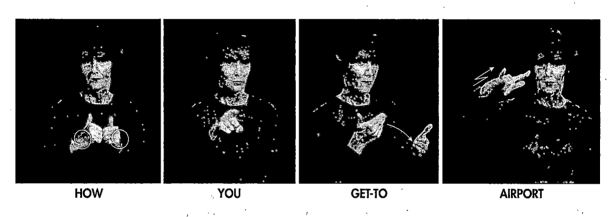

| HOW | YOU | GET-TO | AIRPORT |

English: I think by train.
CS: THINK TRAIN.

| THINK | TRAIN |

English: Why not drive?
CS: WHY NOT DRIVE?

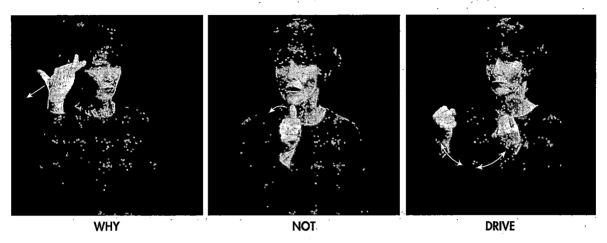

WHY   NOT   DRIVE

English: Maybe the traffic will be bad.
CS: MAYBE TRAFFIC BAD.

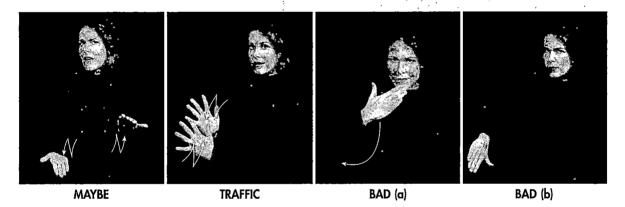

MAYBE   TRAFFIC   BAD (a)   BAD (b)

Additional/Interchangeable Signs

BICYCLE, MOTORCYCLE, RIDE, GARAGE, PARKING

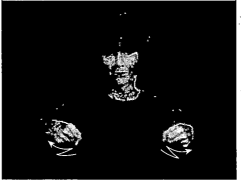

BICYCLE   MOTORCYCLE   RIDE

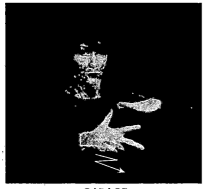

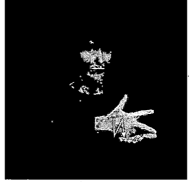

GARAGE   PARKING

Sign On

Note that there are different types and shapes of garages in America, which will influence the formation of the sign GARAGE. Some garages may be in an open space outdoors, some are enclosed, and some are underground. Some garages may have two floors and some may have ten floors (or more)! If this is the case, then sign GARAGE and sign the number of floors by using OPEN B/CLOSED B or BENT B handshape to repeat the number the floors.

Fingerspelled Words

Fingerspell C-A-R or C-R for car, B-U-S for bus, V-A-N for van, T-A-X-I for taxi, C-A-B for taxicabs, F-E-R-R-Y for ferry, and J-E-T for jet.

New Visual-Based Transportation Technology

Announcements made over the speakers cause stress for deaf people! For example, at airports, bus stations, and train stations—not to mention on the plane, and in the bus or train car—announcements are made through speakers to inform passengers of new schedule changes, emergency evacuations, changes of planes, buses, or train cars, and much more. Deaf people rely on visual announcements and appreciate being informed by hearing people if they hear such changes, when visual cues are not available.

Bram Weiser, a computer specialist with the Metropolitan Transportation Authority (MTA) New York City Transit, shares with us the latest visual features included in New York's newest subway cars. For instance, the MTA continues to offer verbal announcements (whether live from train conductors, or as taped recordings), but now also displays electronic signs that visually indicate upcoming stations.

For a customer, these signs continually scroll messages including the subway line she's riding, the train's destination, the station she's

at (or approaching), and the current time of day. They also can show special messages from the conductor for instructions and warnings, such as asking passengers to not hold train doors open while in stations, as that delays train service for everyone.

Another new visual enhancement that these cars have is a lighted "strip map" that shows all of that particular subway line's stations, presented as a row of labeled lights. Passengers can look at the strip map to see lit bulbs to specify the stations yet to be visited, a flashing light for a station that the train is currently at or is approaching, and darkened bulbs that designate stations already visited.

The Least You Need to Know

♦ GPS systems are becoming more popular and widespread, helping people to find their way when they're lost.

♦ Deaf people are excellent drivers and can sign and drive simultaneously.

♦ You learned some signs to use along the way toward a final destination.

♦ Public transportation systems are incorporating visual tools to make travel more accessible for those who can't hear.

In This Chapter

◆ Signs for parts of the body

◆ Signs to communicate that you feel sick

◆ Rights of deaf people in hospitals under the ADA

Chapter 23

I'm Sick

You use the signs in this chapter to sign to someone who is looking a bit under the weather, or if you need to communicate that you're not feeling so good yourself!

We show you signs with which to describe the various aches and pains on your body, and those for illnesses, doctor, hospital, and medical emergency.

Something's Wrong with Me!

Be it a tummy ache or a pain from a surgery, we all feel sick sometimes. It may be a common cold that requires some bed rest at home or a serious illness that requires a trip to the doctor or hospital. In any event, here are some signs that you can use to tell someone that you're not feeling well, or ask about her condition if she's looking sick.

Key Conversational Signs

English: I feel sick.
CS: FEEL SICK.

FEEL

SICK

English: What's wrong?
CS: WHAT-WRONG?

WHAT-WRONG

English: My stomach hurts (aches/pains). Call the hospital.
CS: STOMACH-HURT. PHONE-TO HOSPITAL.

| STOMACH-HURT | PHONE-TO | HOSPITAL (a) | HOSPITAL (b) |

Sign On ___
PHONE-TO is another example of a directional verb sign.

Sign Off ___
Do not use the Y handshape to represent a phone (as shown in the book and DVD) if the person is using a cell phone. The sign will vary and handshapes used may be C to BENT L, depending on the size and type of the cell phone.

Sign On ___
The signs HOSPITAL and DOCTOR vary from region to region. The ones used in the book and DVD are recognized as national signs used in America.

Sign On ___
When you want to show where the pain occurs on the body, sign ACHE near the body part. You can also gesture by pointing (using the number ONE handshape) to indicate where on the body it hurts, and having the expression of pain on your face. In such an emergency situation, obvious/universal gestures such as this may be used to show a cut, a bite, or pain, and can expedite the need for contacting help and showing what needs to be done.

English: The doctor said to go to the Emergency Room!
CS: DOCTOR SAID GO-TO EMERGENCY!

| DOCTOR | SAID | GO-TO | EMERGENCY |

Dr. Dennis Bloomfield, the Associate Dean at New York Medical College, gives advice to health-care workers regarding care of deaf patients:

"The most important tool in the practice of all medicine is the ability to communicate. Up until the last century, when diagnostic technology, effective medications, and safe surgery were developed, communication was the only method of obtaining a working diagnosis, care, and compassion.

In today's technological, automated, test-oriented practice, this communication benefit is often overlooked and the skill forgotten. Deaf patients may be left uninformed, uneasy, and frightened. Medical professionals are encouraged to allow extra time for the consultation, encouraging a longer question-and-answer session so that fears and concerns are properly addressed."

Additional/Interchangeable Signs

HAIR, AMBULANCE, NURSE, MEDICINE, OPERATION (SURGERY), GIVE-AN-INJECTION (INNOCULATION), CUT, BLOOD, DIZZY, VOMIT, WORRY (TROUBLE)

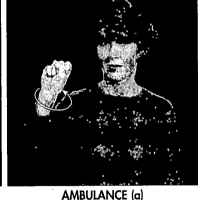

HAIR   AMBULANCE (a)   AMBULANCE (b)

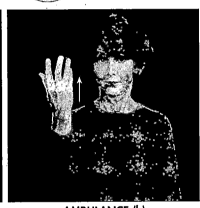

NURSE   MEDICINE   OPERATION (SURGERY)

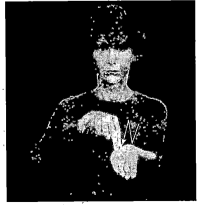

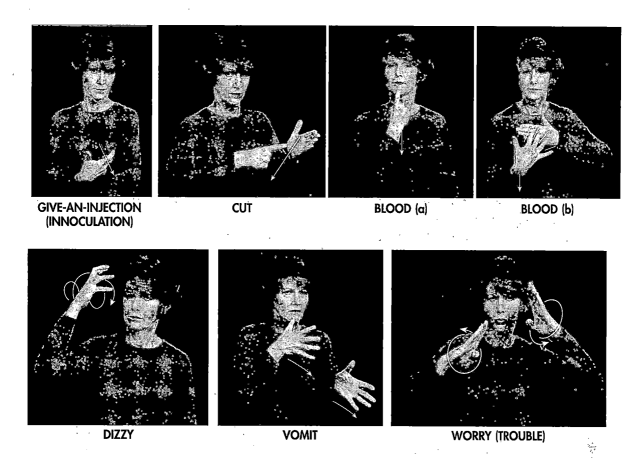

GIVE-AN-INJECTION   CUT   BLOOD (a)   BLOOD (b)
(INNOCULATION)

DIZZY   VOMIT   WORRY (TROUBLE)

Fingerspelled Words

Fingerspell E-R for Emergency Room, C-P-R for cardiopulmonary resuscitation, D-R for doctor, B-U-R-N for burn (when emphasized), and H-R-T for hurt (when emphasized).

ADA Law in Medical Situations

While it is good for you to know these basic medical signs so that you can sign in everyday conversation situations, remember that your vocabulary is not large enough yet to qualify you to interpret in critical medical (such as hospital) situations. Of course, you wouldn't want to miscommunicate important information that could lead to misdiagnosis and improper or delayed medical treatment. The good news is that nowadays hospitals are required under the Americans with Disabilities Act to provide effective means of communication for patients, family members, and hospital visitors who are deaf.

The rights of deaf people in a hospital setting are important for you to know as well, so that you can help them get the services that they are entitled to. The ADA applies to all hospital programs and services, such as emergency-room care, inpatient and outpatient services, surgery, clinics, educational classes, and cafeteria and gift shop services. Wherever patients, their family members, companions, or members of the public are interacting with hospital staff, the hospital is obligated to provide effective communication.

What is considered "effective communication"? The method of communication and the services or aids that the hospital must provide will vary depending upon the abilities of the person who is deaf and on the complexity and nature of the communication that is required. This includes the following:

◆ Exchanging written notes or pointing to items for purchase will likely be effective communication for brief and relatively simple face-to-face conversations, such as a visitor's inquiry about a patient's room number or a purchase in the gift shop or cafeteria.

◆ Written forms or information sheets may provide effective communication in situations where there is little call for interactive communication, such as providing billing and insurance information or filling out admission forms and medical history inquiries.

◆ For more complicated and interactive communications, such as a patient's discussion of symptoms with medical personnel, a physician's presentation of diagnosis and treatment options to patients or family members, or a group therapy session, it may be necessary for the hospital to provide a qualified sign-language interpreter.

Sign Post

The following are situations in which an interpreter may be required for effective communication:

◆ Discussing a patient's symptoms and medical condition, medications, and medical history

◆ Explaining and describing medical conditions, tests, treatment options, medications, surgery, and other procedures

◆ Providing a diagnosis, prognosis, and recommendation for treatment

◆ Obtaining informed consent for treatment

◆ Communicating with a patient during treatment, testing procedures, and during physician's rounds

◆ Providing instructions for medications, post-treatment activities, and follow-up treatments

◆ Providing mental-health services, including group or individual therapy, or counseling for patients and family members

◆ Providing information about blood or organ donations

◆ Explaining living wills and powers of attorney

◆ Discussing complex billing or insurance matters

◆ Making educational presentations, such as birthing and new parent classes, nutrition and weight management counseling, and CPR and first-aid training

Hospitals may also need to provide an interpreter or other assistive service in a variety of situations where it is a patient's family member or friend who is deaf. For example, an interpreter may be necessary to communicate when the guardian of a minor patient is deaf, to discuss prognosis and treatment options with a patient's spouse or partner who is hard-of-hearing, or to allow meaningful participation in a birthing class for a prospective new father who is deaf. Physicians, nurses, laboratory workers, and hospital personnel may also request the assistance of sign-language interpreters.

Sign language or other interpreters must be qualified. An interpreter is qualified if he or she can interpret competently, accurately, and impartially. In the hospital setting, the interpreter must be familiar with any specialized vocabulary used and must be able to interpret medical terms and concepts. Hospital personnel who have a limited familiarity with sign language should comfort and assure a deaf patient through basic signing and gesturing until a qualified interpreter can be present.

Sign Post

Hospitals cannot charge patients or other persons with hearing disabilities an extra fee for interpreter services or other communication aids and services.

◆ For telephone communications, deaf people should be given a teletypewriter (TTY) rather than a standard telephone. The ADA established a free nationwide relay network to handle voice-to-TTY and TTY-to-voice calls. Individuals may use this network to call the hospital from a TTY. The hospital must be prepared to make and receive relay system calls, which may take a little longer than voice calls. For outgoing calls to a TTY user, simply dial 711 to reach a relay operator.

◆ Oral-based deaf people may rely on speechreading hospital staff or require a qualified oral interpreter to assist them in communications.

The Least You Need to Know

◆ Many signs to indicate illness are signed near the body part when the pain occurs.

◆ This chapter taught you signs for common aches and pains and illnesses.

◆ The Americans with Disabilities Act prohibits health-care professionals from discriminating against individuals on the basis of disability, which includes communication.

◆ Under the ADA, hospitals are required to provide effective methods and aids so that deaf patients are able to communicate with doctors, nurses, admission staff, and other hospital workers.

◆ The deaf person chooses the kind of communication that is needed such as sign language through an interpreter, written notes, speechreading, TTYs, or other assistive devices.

In This Chapter

- ◆ Rights of deaf people under federal mandates
- ◆ Deaf jurors
- ◆ Signs for police and fire situations
- ◆ Calling in an emergency

  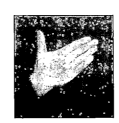  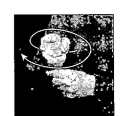

Chapter 24

Emergency/911

We've all become more security-conscious in the United States and look to help others in times of need. It's made us increasingly aware that we all need to help each other to ensure the safety and security of everyone.

In this chapter, you will learn signs to use in communicating with a deaf person in a police or fire situation.

It's the Police!

Imagine if you were surrounded by uniformed officers and car sirens blazing all around you—this would certainly cause anyone to feel panicked. And for a deaf person who has committed a crime, once she is placed in handcuffs, her only means of communication is cut off and she will feel great fear. Having the ability to communicate in sign during law-enforcement scenarios will help to put the deaf person more at ease. The legal system can be very confusing and intimidating.

In the United States, state and local law-enforcement agencies have a federal mandate to ensure appropriate and adequate communication with deaf people. This mandate is found in two federal laws protecting the rights of individuals with disabilities—the Americans with Disabilities Act (ADA) and the Rehabilitation Act of 1973 Section 504 Regulations. Without effective communication in dealing with law-enforcement personnel, serious violations of constitutional and civil rights can occur. Section 504 guarantees nondiscrimination and effective communication for deaf and hard-of-hearing individuals in legal proceedings in state and local courts systems receiving federal funding. The Department of Justice Regulation to Section 504, 28 C.F.R. Part 42, specifically requires the provision of interpreters by courts where necessary to ensure effective communication with a deaf individual. Whether a qualified sign-language interpreter or other auxiliary aid is required depends on the type of communication and the needs of the person. But even if an interpreter is not required, police officers need to take other steps to ensure effective communication, such as writing information and making other accommodations in their usual practices.

 Sign Off

Although we're teaching you some signs for emergency situations, you should not present yourself as a sign-language "interpreter" or sign-language "expert." Help a deaf person who is watching a crime or accident by explaining to her what is going on, but you should not get involved if the deaf person is the criminal. You can tell the police that the person is deaf and ask the person if she needs an interpreter. There are professionals who are nationally certified and highly qualified to perform the role of interpreter in these situations, and it is the deaf person's right to be given this if needed.

For those who have the authority to render the Miranda Rights, remember that the words "You have the right to remain silent …" are familiar to hearing people who may have heard pieces of it in movies, on television, and in school classes (hopefully we haven't heard it first-hand!). But deaf people may not be familiar with these words and following warnings of the Miranda Rights. For this reason, it is important to be especially mindful when it comes to reading the Miranda Rights to a newly arrested deaf person. Finding the best communication method is the top priority. Arranging for a certified interpreter, preferably with a background in criminal law, would be the next step.

Due to the nature of the Miranda Rights, any misunderstanding or misinterpretation of it can be detrimental to the court case proceedings—An innocent person could end up in prison and a felon could go free.

 Sign Post

Before a law-enforcement officer may question you regarding the possible commission of a crime, he must read you the Miranda Rights. He must also make sure that you understand them.

So, while crime and punishment may not be a pleasant subject, here are some signs you can learn regarding law enforcement and police situations.

Key Conversational Signs

English: Look at all the many police officers. What happened?

CS: LOOK-AT MANY POLICE. WHAT-HAPPENED?

 **Sign On**

The sign POLICE also means OFFICER or COP.

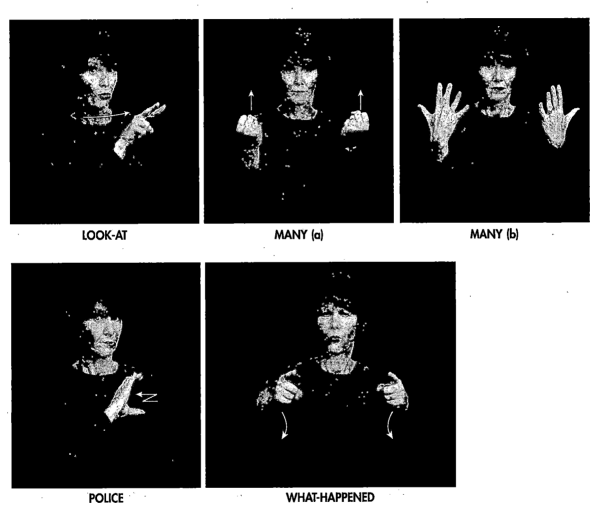

LOOK-AT   MANY (a)   MANY (b)

POLICE   WHAT-HAPPENED

English: The woman was speeding, crashed, and killed a boy.
CS: WOMAN SPEED, CRASH, KILL BOY.

English: They are angry and want her arrested and put in jail.
CS: THEY ANGRY, WANT HER ARREST, PUT-IN JAIL.

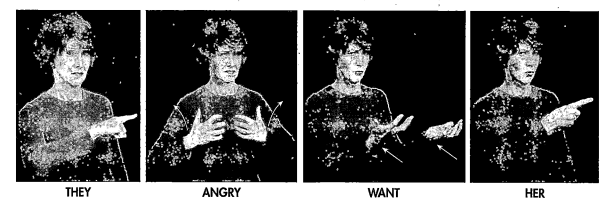

ARREST	PUT-IN	JAIL

Additional/Interchangeable Signs

LICENSE, LAW, WARNING, COURT, JUDGE, PRISON, STEAL, BEATING, AFRAID, GUN, TICKET

ON THE DVD

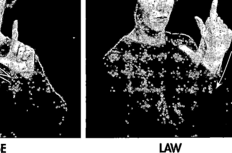

LICENSE	LAW	WARNING

COURT	JUDGE	PRISON

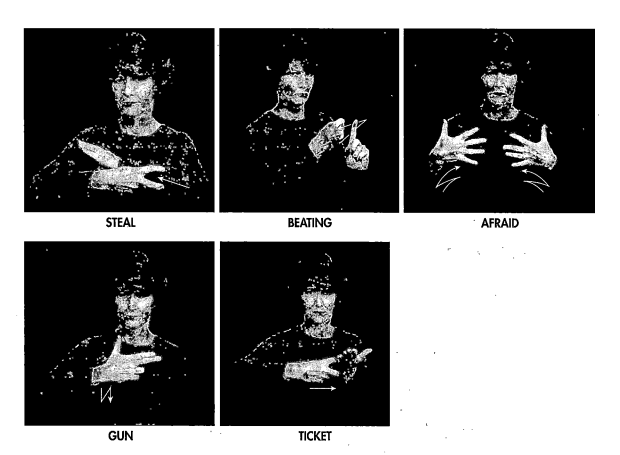

STEAL   BEATING   AFRAID

GUN   TICKET

 Sign On

The sign BEATING shown in the book and DVD is the general sign used to mean that a person is being beaten up. Another way to sign BEATING is to slap your dominant hand on the number "one" handshape formed by your constant hand (or by slapping an area on your body to show specifically where a beating occurred). Another variation is to use your fist with your dominant hand on your body.

Sign Off

Do not use the sign GUN for a rifle; it is used for a pistol or handgun. The sign for GUN varies according to what the device looks like; ask a deaf person the signs for different kinds of guns.

Sign On

Another noun-verb pair is the sign TICKET. If it is signed once, then it means to be ticketed (to get a ticket) as shown in the book and DVD. If it is signed twice, it becomes a noun (e.g., a ticket used to gain entrance to an event).

Fingerspelled Words

Fingerspell G-U-N for gun, K-I-L-L for kill or murder, and R-A-P-E for rape.

Sign Post

There is a resource center for battered deaf women in the Bay Area, CA, called DeafHope. DeafHope's mission is to provide their clients with support services such as counseling, shelter referrals, and legal assistance. Volunteers also train shelters on how to make their services available to deaf women in American Sign Language. DeafHope legal advocate Jane Whitney, herself deaf, got involved in the former Deaf Women Against Violence after her best friend was killed by an ex-boyfriend. Whitney now helps deaf clients get restraining orders, works on child custody issues, and navigates deaf women through what can be an otherwise intimidating legal system.

Deaf People as Jurors

Deaf people can also serve as jurors in the Unites States court system. Under the ADA, local and state courts are prohibited from excluding persons from jury service based on deafness. Title II of the ADA states: *No qualified individual with a disability shall, by reason of such disability, be excluded from participation in or be denied the benefits of the services, programs, or activities of a public entity, or be subjected to discrimination by any such entity.* The court systems are required to provide qualified sign-language interpreters and other auxiliary aids to ensure that deaf people can serve as jurors effectively.

Fire!

Quick recognition that someone is deaf is important to make sure that appropriate actions are taken in fire emergency situations. Sometimes in a crisis, it's easy to forget that not everybody can hear you. If you suspect that someone is deaf, sign to her and ask if she is deaf, or use gestures by pointing to her and then to your ear and shake your head "no" (meaning "not hearing"). Her life may depend on communication taking place without delay.

Firefighters are prepared for all kinds of fire emergencies, but much of the time they handle other kinds of emergencies, including medical, accidents, and disasters. Firefighters generally do not receive formal training to communicate with deaf people (although an increasing number of areas are trying to provide educational programs for them). As you can imagine, there are many cases for which emergencies must be handled as quickly as possible. Any helpful information that you can give the firefighter will give the impacted person a better chance for safety and/or recovery.

Fire, emergency, and unexpected weather warnings are now available through a pager system at worksites. The pagers are connected to the main operating system. In the event of a fire or other emergency, the operator types the information into the system and sends out the message. The pagers vibrate, warning the employee to check the message. The text pagers tell the employee where the emergency is, whether it's in her workplace or elsewhere. Also, there are other systems readily available, such as fire alarm strobe-light devices. If the fire alarm goes off in the building, the light flashes.

Sign On

When it comes to emergency, deaf people may ask you to call for help. Dialing 9-1-1 in the United States (and some parts of Canada) will connect you to a dispatcher who can quickly route your call to local emergency medical, fire, and law-enforcement agencies. If a deaf person is home, she will use a paper or TTY and call 9-1-1 directly, as the dispatchers have TTY services as well.

Now you will learn some signs you can use in the event of a fire emergency.

Key Conversational Signs

English: I smell smoke and can't breathe.
CS: SMELL SMOKE, CAN'T BREATHE.

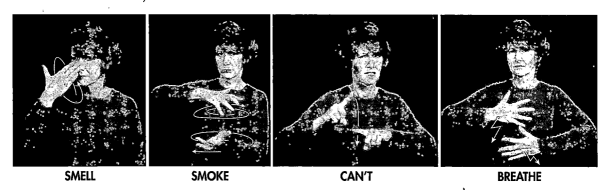

SMELL	SMOKE	CAN'T	BREATHE

English: Find the fire escape.
CS: FIND FIRE ESCAPE.

FIND (a)	FIND (b)	FIRE	ESCAPE

English: The ladder is over there.
CS: LADDER OVER-THERE.

LADDER	OVER-THERE

Additional/Interchangeable Signs

BREAK, PULL, PUSH, FIREFIGHTER

| BREAK | PULL | PUSH | FIREFIGHTER |

Fingerspelled Words

Fingerspell E-M-T for emergency medical technician, T-R-U-C-K or T-R-C-K for truck, E-X-I-T for exit, R-U-N for run (when emphasized), and G-O for go (when emphasized).

The Least You Need to Know

◆ The Americans with Disabilities Act and the Rehabilitation Act are federal mandates that protect deaf people's rights in law enforcement situations.

◆ Trained and certified sign-language interpreters are qualified to interpret in legal situations.

◆ Deaf people can serve as jurors and perform jury duty, and are provided with a professional sign-language interpreter.

◆ Communication with a deaf person could help to save his or her life in a fire or other life-threatening disaster.

◆ In America, 9-1-1 is the phone number used for both hearing and TTY emergency calls.

In This Part

Part

You're Off and Signing!

We end the book by giving you some ideas for what to do if you're in a conversation with a deaf person and aren't sure if your message is coming across clearly. We also give tips for you to practice and suggest additional resources for further reading and study.

We hope we've whet your appetite and that you'll continue to learn sign language and Deaf culture and to socialize with deaf signers. And now you're off and signing!

In This Chapter

- ◆ Making sure your message is understood
- ◆ Troubleshooting for communication breakdowns
- ◆ Signs for clarification
- ◆ What to do if you're feeling "stuck"

Chapter **25**

Are We Clear?

You're now well on your way to having basic conversations with deaf people! You may still be building your confidence level while you're learning, but remember—You CAN do it! For some people, signing comes more easily than it does for others. That's okay. We've all been raised differently, and have different comfort levels with expressing ourselves with our faces, bodies, and hands. As you become comfortable signing, you'll see that all these things are a natural part of communication (in any language!).

In this chapter, we discuss what to do when you're not sure about the clarity of your message while engaged in dialogue with a deaf person. Remember, the goal is to communicate! You may think that you're "stuck" and begin to feel nervous, intimidated, or frustrated, but before you hit the panic button, we give you some ideas to make sure you can have a great, meaningful conversation!

Am I Making Myself Clear?

Just as when you talk to another hearing person, sometimes you miss what a deaf person is trying to communicate. Don't panic. You've got your foot in the door ... keep it open! Most deaf people have patience with new signers—They appreciate that you're trying to initiate interaction. The most important thing is your willingness and desire to communicate. Positive attitude always wins!

If a deaf person has missed the gist of your message, you can try some techniques that you already use with other hearing people whose first language is English. Remember, the deaf person is the expert with her language, while you are reaching out (brilliantly and boldly) to cross a language barrier.

◆ Repeat what you signed, but change the speed. If you signed too quickly, go slower. Too slow? Try it faster.

◆ Rephrase what you signed, or choose different signs altogether.

◆ Keep it simple. Remember that you do not yet have an extensive vocabulary to discuss topics in depth.

Checking for Understanding

There may be times when you are uncertain about the clarity of your message, or just want to check to make sure that the deaf person understands what you're trying to convey. Go right ahead and ask her—It will make you both more at ease knowing that you're communicating well together.

Here are some sample conversations and new signs to help you ask about clarity of your message.

Key Conversational Phrases Include

English: Do you understand me?
CS: UNDERSTAND ME?

UNDERSTAND (a)

UNDERSTAND (b)

ME

English: No, I am not clear. Please repeat.
CS: NO, NOT-CLEAR. PLEASE REPEAT.

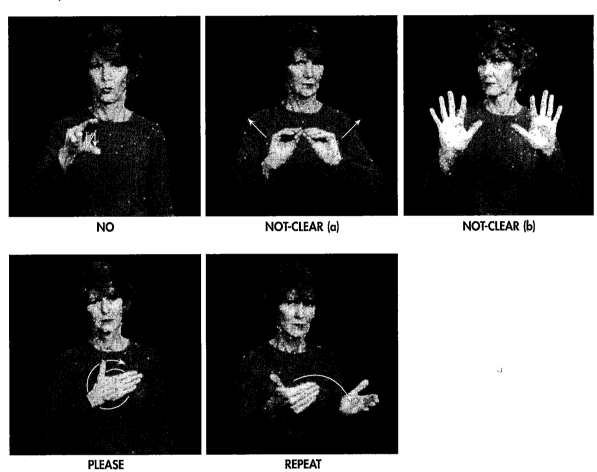

English: Okay, I am going to try again.
CS: O-K, TRY AGAIN.

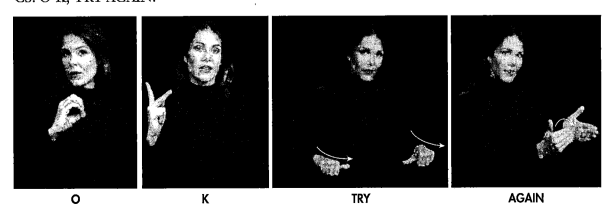

Additional/Interchangeable Signs

SLOW, FAST, PRACTICE

| SLOW | FAST (a) | FAST (b) | PRACTICE |

Fingerspelled Words

Fingerspell O-H for oh, and Y-E-S for yes (when emphasized).

SOS: Use Gestures

Ideally, you'll be able to combine signing and fingerspelling to get your message across. But what if you don't know or aren't sure of the sign but still want to get your point across? You can use gestures, or a blend of signs and gestures. Gestures are a natural part of all languages— spoken or visual.

You already use gestures everyday. You wave your hand to mean "hello" or "goodbye"; use the V handshape to mean "victory" or "peace"; the F handshape to mean "everything's a-okay," "all's fine," or "yes"; and an upright A hand-shape to mean "good work," "good job," or "ready ... let's do it." You use gestures to show action, too. For example, you may put your hands to your mouth and simulate blowing a whistle. Or you may indicate that you are hot by simulating wiping sweat off your forehead and fanning your face and body. Another very common gesture in America is holding your palm up and wiggling your forefinger at some-one as if to mean, "Come here."

Additionally, pointing to objects or people can be helpful. In America, we usually use a finger (NUMBER ONE handshape) toward the intended object or person. Although you may have been brought up hearing that "it's not polite to point," it is acceptable in the Deaf culture.

Other Ideas for Alternative Visual Communication

Wait ... there's no need to give up and walk away. In the unlikely event that the methods above don't work, or if you're just not comfort-able with using signs in live conversation yet, just keep going with your dialogue by using other methods. You can continue practicing signing before you see your deaf friend, neigh-bor, co-worker, or family member the next time you meet.

If you are feeling a little frustrated, your fin-gers are cramping and you need to take a break, ask your communication partner for a short-term alternative in communication. Here are some options for what you could do:

◆ Use paper and pen to write notes. If you do this, keep your sentences simple and short.

Sign Off

Don't rely too heavily on writing your message on paper ... this could be seen as a cop-out!

- ◆ Computers are a way to communicate, too. With instant messages and e-mails, chatting can be cyber-licious!
- ◆ Use a sign-language interpreter. Remember that when using an interpreter, look at the deaf person and maintain eye contact with her—She is the one with whom you want to share the story! The interpreter is the live conduit of conversation between the two of you.
- ◆ Use clear speech if the person can speechread. Again, remember that less than 30 percent of speech can be read correctly. For this reason, speechreading is often the least favorable method of alternate communication.

Of course, when you have a chance, you should review your signs with the photos in this book or view the demonstrations in the DVD. Were your handshapes correct when you were trying to make the sign? How about your palm orientations and hand movements and locations? Think about your facial expressions and body movements. Were they in sync with what you're trying to convey? Feedback is important. Enlist a friend or family and learn together!

Remember, the goal here is to communicate! Sharing a message, delivering information, and conveying a thought are the goals. Don't feel discouraged. You're learning a new communication mode and this takes time. You're already opening the lines of communication and that's a great thing!

The Least You Need to Know

- ◆ Repeat, rephrase, or summarize what you signed if it wasn't clear the first time.
- ◆ Ask the deaf person if you are being clear; ask how the communication could be better.
- ◆ Use both signs and fingerspelling to get your message across. Gestures, or a blend of signs and gestures, can also be helpful in communicating your point.
- ◆ Don't give up on the conversation! Find the best method of direct communication with the deaf person.

In This Chapter

◆ Don't forget what you just learned!

◆ Keep on learning

◆ Practice tips—by yourself or with a friend

◆ Resources for further studies

Chapter **26**

Keep Going!

It's no secret: The key to becoming proficient in signing is to keep on practicing. Like anything, the more you use what you know, the more you will retain in your long-term memory. With practice, you'll even become more comfortable with your facial and body expressions, optimizing your hand flexibility, and becoming more creative with your signs and use of gesturing. While it is important to fine-tune what you already know, continue expanding your sign vocabulary. You will ultimately rely less and less on gestures.

In this chapter, we share with you tips so you can practice what we've shown you. And we demonstrate ways to continue learning sign language if you so desire (and we hope it is your desire to keep on going)!

Practice What You Know

You don't want to forget what you've already learned! Practice, practice, practice, so that your muscles will remember as well as your brain. Over time, you'll get faster at delivering your signs.

As a visual mode of communication, sign language is different from any other auditory language. Recognize that you need to adjust to the mind-shift here. You'll be using your eyes, not your ears. You'll be using your hands, not your vocal cords. You'll be using parts of your face and body more than you have before. All this takes time to get used to.

Here are some ideas to help you practice your signs:

◆ Practice your facial expressions using a mirror. How do you show fear, happiness, anger, frustration, confusion, or intensity? Say to yourself, I am feeling this XYZ emotion right now (pick one!), and then show it!

◆ Practice with a friend. Using the conversation dialogues in the book, one of you would play the role of Carole and sign her sentences, and the other take the role of Dawn and sign her sentences. When you've completed your "signing parts," reverse roles and sentences!

◆ Use the DVD and sign along with Carole and Dawn as they show you how to put it all together for signing handshapes, the alphabet, numbers, basic signs, conversational dialogues, and additional interchangeable signs. You'll be able to pause the DVD, review, and practice again and again as much as you need until your muscles and brain have these committed to memory.

◆ Write down each of the words found in the Index of Signs on index cards ... writing one word per card. Mix up the deck of cards and pick out a word. Try and sign it. Did you get it right? Check the page the sign is on in the book or DVD.

◆ Describe the world around you in sign. Fingerspell words you see as you go about your day. Then, go ahead and try to sign the same words.

Learn What You Don't Know

Purchase a sign-language dictionary. The most comprehensive ones will have between 5,000 and 7,000 signs. You'll be able to practice a lot! Try to sign the words in a newspaper or magazine or book. Stuck on a word? Look it up in the sign-language dictionary. Remember, there isn't a sign for every English word, so you'll see the same sign to mean more than just one word in English. You may want to buy more than one sign-language dictionary, as you'll see that different books will have different versions of signs (because signs can vary regionally).

Four well-rated sign-language dictionaries are ...

◆ *The American Sign Language Handshape Dictionary* by Richard A. Tennant, Marianne Gluszak Brown

◆ *Gallaudet Survival Guide to Signing* by Leonard G. Lane

◆ *American Sign Language Dictionary Unabridged* by Martin L. Sternberg

◆ *Random House Webster's American Sign Language Dictionary* by Elaine Costello

Hands-down, the best way to learn sign-language (especially American Sign Language) is through a course taught by a deaf person. Many community colleges offer ASL courses through their department of continuing education (or "extension programs"). Courses usually last around 12 to 15 weeks for a first-level course. You can start by using the yellow pages and making inquiries of your local community colleges.

Sign On _____

There are lots of places in your residential area that offer sign-language instruction—from private tutorial sessions to general classes held at schools, universities, churches, and institutions. Pick up your local newspapers or phone yellow pages for more information.

If you live in the vicinity of a residential school for the deaf, they'll also usually offer classes for those learning ASL, which are often geared to the friends and family of deaf people.

An excellent and time-effective way to learn ASL is through intensive, "total immersion" courses. Washington D.C.'s Gallaudet University's summer ASL courses are considered by many renowned experts in the field to be one of the best. The student is immersed in Deaf culture and language during his semester. Gallaudet's summer program begins mid-June and lasts through mid-August and is reasonably priced (especially the tuition, room, and board package).

Read books focused on Deaf culture and Deaf experiences. Here are some highly recommended ones (and very popular and topical ones among deaf and hearing communities!) that you may choose to put toward the top of your reading list …

◆ *Deaf in America: Voices from a Culture* by Carol Padden, Tom Humphries (Contributor)
◆ *The Mask of Benevolence: Disabling the Deaf Community* by Harlan Lane
◆ *Deaf Like Me* by Thomas Spradley and James Spradley

◆ *A Deaf Adult Speaks Out* by Leo Jacobs
◆ *When the Mind Hears* by Harlan Lane
◆ *A Journey into the Deaf-World* by Harlan Lane, Robert Hoffmeister, and Benjamin Behan
◆ *Odyssey of Hearing Loss: Tales of Triumph* by Michael A. Harvey
◆ *Everyone Here Spoke Sign Language: Hereditary Deafness on Martha's Vineyard* by Nora Ellen Groce, John W. M. Whiting
◆ *Train Go Sorry: Inside a Deaf World* by Leah Hager Cohen
◆ *Seeing Voices: Journey into the World of the Deaf* by Oliver Sacks

Explore ASL videos. Dawn Sign Press has a popular video and workbook series called "Signing Naturally." Also, there are "Say it by Signing" videos created by Elaine Costello.

Observe fluent signers and be aware of their facial expressions, body language, and handshapes. You may watch fluent signers engaged in conversation on a street, or attend an interpreted theatrical performance in your area. These days, almost all performances have at least one evening when they are interpreted in sign language. Call the box office to see when these special signed performances are held. Also, find out when the National Theatre of the Deaf and the Deafwest Theatre Company may be touring in your area.

Volunteer at events where sign language will be used. These are wonderful and fun ways to gain exposure to sign language. You'll be able to practice real-time, short conversations. And you will most likely see professional American Sign Language interpreters who are wonderful to observe.

Watch some Deaf-related movies. You can go to your nearest library, video store, or Blockbuster and pick these up, or order them online, too. Some great movies to check out include ...

- ◆ *Children of a Lesser God*
- ◆ *Love Is Never Silent*
- ◆ *Mr. Holland's Opus*
- ◆ *Land Before Time*
- ◆ *What the Deaf Man Heard*
- ◆ *In the Land of the Deaf*
- ◆ *Beyond Silence*
- ◆ *Breaking Through*
- ◆ *Bridge to Silence*
- ◆ *And Your Name is Jonah*
- ◆ *Dummy*
- ◆ *Johnnie Belinda*
- ◆ *Choices*
- ◆ *Dead Silence*

Go online and use the Internet to visit Deaf/ASL-related websites, many of which contain animated dictionaries, stories about Deaf culture, news stories, and poems. A list of these websites can be found in Appendix B.

A Few Last Words

So now you've read the book and watched the DVD! Congratulations. You have learned the basic signs that will facilitate conversations with deaf people in a variety of scenarios. Maybe you've had an opportunity to use some of what you've learned already. Or, maybe you're just about to get out there and start signing.

Remember, do not get discouraged! Learning a new way to communicate is a process and everyone makes mistakes. Nothing worthwhile comes instantaneously—Have patience and keep building your signing skills! You can succeed in developing your communication repertoire with deaf people using Contact Signing. Good luck and ENJOY!

Highest regards,

Your signing friends—Carole and Dawn

The Least You Need to Know

- ◆ Keep on practicing what you've already learned by referring back to this book and DVD, describing the world around you as you go about your day, and enlisting a friend to sign along with you.
- ◆ Expand your knowledge by buying a comprehensive sign dictionary, taking a sign-language or ASL courses, watching fluent signers, or purchasing Deaf-related books, videos, and movies.
- ◆ It's a challenge to go from using an auditory language to using a visual language, but soon you'll have communication skills and strategies using your senses in a new and exciting way!

Glossary

American Manual Alphabet Comprised of 26 handshapes representing the 26 letters of the English alphabet; used to spell words.

Americans with Disabilities Act (ADA) A federal law signed in 1990 that bans discrimination based on disability in the areas of public accommodations, state and local government services, employment, transportation, and telecommunications. Known as a "civil rights act for persons with disabilities," the ADA requires public services and buildings to make reasonable accommodations to provide access to persons with disabilities, including those with hearing losses.

American Sign Language (ASL) ASL is considered by the Deaf community to be the natural, visual language of deaf people. It has its own syntax and grammatical structure (different from English) and is the third most used language in the United States. The placement, movement, and expression of the hands, face, and body are part of the language.

bilingual/bicultural Having fluency in two languages and membership in two cultures, such as Deaf culture membership and use of sign language, and hearing culture membership and use of spoken language.

Children of Deaf Adults (CODA) Hearing children of deaf parent(s).

cochlear implant An electronic device that is surgically implanted into the inner ear, the cochlea. When sounds are received through a transducer, an external device that has a microphone, it sends signals to the device that stimulate it to cause hearing of sounds.

contact signing Method of communication most commonly used when hearing people and deaf people come into contact with each other. CS utilizes ASL signs and some grammatical principles, while mostly holding English word order.

closed caption   A text display of words and sounds presented on a television, video, or movie screen that enables a deaf viewer to simultaneously follow the dialogue and the action of a program. By law, 13-inch-or-larger televisions manufactured after 1993 must have closed-caption capability.

deaf   Deaf with a small "d" means a person who has a hearing loss, such that she is unable to understand or process linguistic information through hearing without the use of an assistive device. Communication and learning for a deaf person may be primarily through visual methods (e.g., manual communication, writing, speechreading, and gestures). Also, in this book, "deaf" includes hard-of-hearing people who may face communication barriers.

Deaf   Deaf with a capital "D" means a person who considers herself belonging to the Deaf culture and community, and chooses to communicate using American Sign Language.

Deaf community   A group of people who share common interests, heritage, and language (ASL). The United States Deaf community encompasses individuals who have a broad range of perspectives relating to Deaf issues, yet remains certain on deafness as a positive state of being.

Deaf culture   A capital "D" is often used in the word Deaf when it relates to the cultural aspects of deafness. The Deaf culture is a learned, shared, and constantly evolving system of values, beliefs, and standards that guide deaf people's thoughts, feelings, and behaviors. Some of the central components of Deaf culture include the use of American Sign Language, social interaction with other individuals who are deaf, and involvement in Deaf organizations. The Deaf culture places a high value on its language (ASL), social relationships with other deaf people and Deaf organizations, art forms (storytelling, poetry, drama), and stories and literature about deaf people.

decibel (dB)   The unit that measures the intensity of a sound. The higher the dB level, the more intense the sound, and the more severe the hearing loss.

fingerspelling   Uses the 26 letters of the American Manual alphabet. Fingerspelling is usually used for proper nouns and other specific information (e.g., place names, brand names, and titles).

Gallaudet University   Located in Washington, D.C., the only liberal arts university in the world designed for deaf, hard-of-hearing, and hearing students. The University offers undergraduate and graduate academic programs, along with national elementary and secondary education programs. Gallaudet is a leading authority on many topics related to deafness and Deaf culture.

gesture   Movements of the hands or body to convey an idea. They may be used alone or in combination with signs to communicate thoughts. Common gestures include pointing, head nodding, and waving "goodbye."

handshapes   Formation of the fingers and palm(s) when producing a sign. Many of the ASL handshapes stem from the American Manual Alphabet and manual numbers.

hard-of-hearing   A person with a mild degree of hearing loss. Some hard-of-hearing individuals use hearing aids or other assistive-listening devices. They might speak by using their voice, and might speechread.

hearing aid   An electronic device that conducts and amplifies sound to the ear. It is a removable device, which generally consists of a microphone, amplifier, and receiver. Sound might be heard through an ear mold worn in the ear. Hearing aids do not distinguish between desired sounds (a message) and unwanted sounds (background noises).

hearing loss   Levels of hearing loss are generally regarded as follows:

- ◆ Normal Hearing: 0 dB to 15 dB
- ◆ Mild Loss: 16 dB to 35 dB
- ◆ Moderate: 36 dB to 50 dB
- ◆ Moderate–Severe: 51 dB to 70 dB
- ◆ Severe: 71 dB to 90 dB
- ◆ Profound: 91 dB or more

mainstreaming   One of the educational options for deaf children, which takes place in certain public schools around the country. Mainstreaming is the concept that deaf students should be integrated into classes with hearing peers to the maximum extent possible.

National Association of the Deaf (NAD) Located in Maryland, the oldest and largest constituency organization safeguarding the accessibility and civil rights for deaf people in the United States. NAD is a private, nonprofit organization.

palm orientation   Direction that the palm(s) faces when making a sign.

presbycusis   Hearing loss that occurs naturally due to the aging process.

relay telephone services/relay network A service that involves a third-party operator who "relays" a conversation between a deaf person (who uses a TTY) and a hearing/speaking person (who uses an ordinary, non-adapted phone).

sign language   Any number of methods of communication used by deaf people in which hand and body movements, gestures, and facial expressions convey grammatical structure and meaning.

sign-language interpreter   A person who facilitates communication between deaf and hearing people through interpretation of sign language and spoken language.

signed English   Sign systems that use manual signs in English word order, and English grammatical structure and syntax.

speechreading   The practice of reading speech of a person by observing lip movements, lip patterns, and facial expressions. Formerly known as lipreading, this is correctly referred to as speechreading. Even for very skilled speechreaders, only about 30 percent of spoken languages can be understood through speechreading.

TTY (Teletypewriter)   Also known as a text telephone, this device transmits and receives typewritten messages via regular phone lines. A TTY has a keyboard (to type messages) and a screen (to view messages).

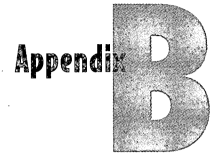

Appendix **B**

Web Resources

The Internet offers a great wealth of information and resources pertaining to deaf, hard-of-hearing, and deaf-blind. We selected the following websites to give you a good start in your research as you continue to learn more about these exciting and interesting topics!

Cultural Arts and Entertainment

Deaf West Theatre
www.deafwest.org

Based in Los Angeles, this is one of the newest theaters in America. It featured a multi-award-winning Broadway show, *Big River*, along with the RoundAbout Theatre Company.

National Theatre of the Deaf
www.ntd.org

The oldest touring theater company in America. It has given at least 62 national tours in all 50 states, 30 international tours, and over 7,000 performances.

Cultural Calendars

ASLinfo.com
www.aslinfo.com

Provides a calendar of cultural Deaf events in Florida, such as silent dinners, silent coffee nights, Deaf nights, and many others.

Community Outreach Program for the Deaf
www.copdnm.org

This New Mexico organization provides a calendar of Deaf cultural events.

Hands On
www.handson.org

Posts a monthly calendar that lists Deaf arts and cultural events in New York City.

Deaf News

Deaf Nation
www.deafnation.com

Gives news, articles, and information about current events and offerings.

DeafToday
www.deaftoday.com

Brings you daily news from around the world.

Diverse Deaf Communities

American Association of the Deaf-Blind
www.aadb.org

A national consumer advocacy for deaf-blind individuals that provides information, technical assistance, and resources.

Deaf Women United
www.dwu.org

An organization that is of, for, and by deaf women. It focuses on advocacy, education, and outreach.

National Asian Deaf Congress
www.nadc-usa.org

Addresses the cultural, political, and social issues experienced by Asians who are deaf or hard-of-hearing. NADC strives to provide education, empowerment, and leadership for its members and member organizations.

National Black Deaf Advocates
www.nbda.org

Promotes Deaf awareness and leadership, as well as active participation in the political, educational, and economic developments of American black deaf citizens. There are approximately 28 chapters in the United States and the Virgin Islands.

Rainbow of the Deaf
www.rad.org

A national organization with approximately 24 chapters in North America serving gay, lesbian, and bisexual people who are deaf and hard-of-hearing.

Education

Postsecondary Education Programs Network (PEPNet)
www.pepnet.org

Here's a website that offers a free online course about the basics of deafness. You'll even receive a certificate upon completion! Once on the website, click Orientation to Serving College Students Who are Deaf or Hard-of-Hearing. PEPNet is comprised of four regional centers, and aims to assist postsecondary institutions in America by providing information and resources.

General Information

Laurent Clerc National Deaf Education Center
www.clerccenter.gallaudet.edu

Offers a diverse range of information covering issues and topics related to deafness, education, and resources.

The Deaf Resource Library
www.deaflibrary.org

A virtual library containing a collection of reference material and links regarding Deaf culture and other related topics about deaf and hard-of hearing people in America and overseas.

Interpreter Organizations

Conference of Interpreter Trainers
www.cit-asl.org

Promotes quality education for interpreters working with American Sign Language and English.

National Alliance of Black Interpreters
www.naobi.org

Promotes excellence and empowerment among African Americans/Blacks in the profession of sign-language interpreting.

Registry of Interpreters for the Deaf
www.rid.org

Offers national, regional, state, and local forums. It serves as an organizational structure for the continued growth and development of the professions of interpretation and transliteration of American Sign Language and English. It also provides national certificate examinations.

Law

ADA Homepage
www.ada.gov

A government website that offers information and technical assistance about the Americans with Disabilities Act.

National Organizations

American Society for Deaf Children
www.deafchildren.org

A nonprofit organization promoting a positive attitude toward signing, as well as providing information and resources for deaf children.

Children of Deaf Adults
www.coda-international.org

A nonprofit organization for hearing sons and daughters of deaf parents.

Cochlear Implant Association, Inc
www.cici.org

Provides advocacy, support, and information regarding cochlear implants. It was formerly known as the Cochlear Implant Club International.

Helen Keller National Center for Deaf-Blind Youths and Adults
www.hknc.org

A national center with 10 regional offices to provide comprehensive services, information, and resources.

League for the Hard of Hearing
www.lhh.org

Provides comprehensive hearing rehabilitation and human services, as well as education and research programs.

National Association of the Deaf
www.nad.org

The largest organization safeguarding the accessibility and civil rights of deaf and hard-of-hearing Americans in education, employment, health care, and telecommunications.

Resources for Skill Development

Dawn Sign Press
www.dawnsign.com

Offers educational and entertaining materials and products related to Deaf culture and American Sign Language.

Harris Communications
www.harriscomm.com

Offers products ranging from devices to books and videotapes.

Signs of Development
www.signs-of-development.org

Offers distance education, professional development, workshops, mentoring, and educational materials for interpreters, educators, students, and signers.

Sign-Language Teacher Organization

American Sign Language Teachers Association
www.aslta.org

Promotes quality education, evaluation, certification standards, and procedures for sign-language teachers. For those sign-language teachers (or teachers-to-be), this website is for you.

Sports

USA Deaf Sports Federation
www.usadsf.org

Governing body for all Deaf sports and recreation in the United States. It sponsors the Deaf U.S. team in the World Games for the Deaf and other regional, national, and international competitions. To learn more about local or regional sports events, look at websites that may be created by those in your home region such as Wisconsin Deaf Sports Club (www.wi-deafsports.org) or Austin Deaf Club (www.austindeafclub.org).

National Deaf Bowling Association and the **National Deaf Women's Bowling Association**
www.ndba-ndwba.com

For bowlers and their fans.

The United States Deaf Golf Foundation
www.usdgf.org

Promotes championship golf among deaf individuals. There are also local golf associations in states such as New Jersey (www.sjdga.com), Ohio (www.odga.info), and South Carolina (www.scdga.org).

Deaf Pilots Association
www.deafpilots.com

For active pilots and aircraft owners alike.

Technology

Telecommunications for the Deaf, Inc.
www.tdi-online.org

Promotes equal access to telecommunications and media. It is a nonprofit consumer advocacy organization providing resources about local relay services in your home area.

National relay centers
www.consumer.att.com/relay/
www.ip-relay.com
www.relaycall.com
www.sprintrelayonline.com

Captioned Media Program
www.cfv.org

A free-loan open-captioned media program for deaf and hard-of-hearing persons, teachers, parents, and others. Videos and DVDs include educational, general, and special-interest topics.

National Captioning Institute
www.ncicap.org

The largest provider of closed-captioned television services for the broadcast, cable, and home-video industry.

Index